SO-AHG-842

# One Word From God Can Change Your Destiny

*By Kenneth and Gloria Copeland*

Harrison House
Tulsa, Oklahoma

*One Word From God Can Change Your Destiny*

30-0715

All rights reserved. No part of this book may be reproduced or transmitted in any form or by any means, electronic or mechanical, including photocopying, recording, or by any information storage and retrieval system, without the written permission of the publisher. Printed in the United States of America.

07 06 05 04 03 02 01 00 99      10 9 8 7 6 5 4 3 2

All Scripture is from the *King James Version* unless otherwise noted as the following:

*The Amplified Bible, Old Testament* copyright © 1965, 1987 by The Zondervan Corporation. *The Amplified New Testament* copyright © 1958, 1987 by The Lockman Foundation. Used by permission.

*New King James Version,* copyright © 1982 by Thomas Nelson, Inc.

*The Holy Bible, New International Version,* copyright © 1973, 1978, 1884 by the International Bible Society. Used by permission of Zondervan Publishing House.

*New American Standard Bible*®, copyright © 1960, 1962, 1963, 1968, 1971, 1972, 1973, 1975, 1977, 1994 by the Lockman Foundation. Used by permission.

*New Testament in Modern English,* J.B. Phillips, copyright © J.B. Phillips 1958, 1959, 1960, 1972.

*The Living Bible,* copyright © 1971. Used by permission of Tyndale House Publishers Inc., Wheaton, Illinois 60189. All rights reserved.

*One Word From God Can Change Your Destiny*
ISBN 1-57794-147-0
Copyright © 1999 by Kenneth and Gloria Copeland
Kenneth Copeland Ministries
Fort Worth, Texas 76192-0001

Published by Harrison House, Inc.
P.O. Box 35035
Tulsa, Oklahoma 74153

# Contents

# Introduction

## One Word From God Can Change Your Life FOREVER!

When the revelation of this statement exploded on the inside of me, it changed the way I think...about everything! I had been praying for several days about a situation that seemed at the time to be overwhelming. I had been confessing the Word of God over it, but that Word had begun to come out of my head and not my heart. I was pushing in my flesh for the circumstance to change. As I made my confession one more time, the Spirit of God seemed to say to me, *Why don't you be quiet?!*

I said, "But Lord, I'm confessing the Word!"

He answered inside me, *I know it. I heard you. Now just be still and be quiet a little while, and let the Word of God settle down in your spirit. Quit trying to make this thing happen. You're not God.*

*You're not going to be the one to make it happen anyway!*

So I stopped. I stopped in that situation in my mind and began to get quiet before the Lord...and this phrase came up in my spirit..."**One word from God can change anything.**"

So I started saying that. I said it off and on all day. It came easily because it came from God—not from my own thinking.

Every time I was tempted to worry or think of ideas concerning my circumstances, I'd think, *Yes, just one word from God...*

I noticed when I'd say that, **the peace of God** would come on me. It was so calming. As a result, a habit developed in me. People would bring me issues. They'd say, "Well, what about..." And I'd either say aloud or think to myself, **"Yeah, that may be so, but one word from God will change anything.**"

It began to be the answer for everything. If I was watching television and the newscaster was telling about a disaster, and the people being interviewed were saying things to the effect of "Oh, what are we going to do? It's all been blown away, burned up or shook up...," I'd say, **"Yeah, but one word from God can change anything."**

It really developed into a strength for me and it can for you. That's why we've put together the **One Word From God Book Series**...there could be just one word in these inspiring articles that can change your outlook on life forever.

You've been searching, seeking help...and God has the answer. He has the one word that can turn your circumstance around and put you on dry ground. He has the one word that gives you all the peace that's in Him. He is your Father. He wants you to rejoice in your right-standing with Him. He wants you to know that He has plans for you, plans to prosper you and not to harm you, plans to give you hope and a future. (Jeremiah 29:11)

God loves you. And He has a word for you. One Word that can change your life FOREVER!

*Kenneth Copeland*

## Chapter 1

# Hope: The Blueprint of Faith

*"Where there is no vision, the people perish."*
— PROVERBS 29:18

Kenneth Copeland

If I asked you to explain to me what hope is, what would you say? What example would you give me from your own life?

Would you think back to a time when you hoped for something...just to have those hopes dissolve into disappointment?

Most people would. That's because, in their minds, hope and disappointment keep very close company. Such close company, in fact, that even the word itself, "hope," has a ring of uncertainty. "Maybe it will happen—maybe it won't," they say. "All we can do is hope."

But there's something very wrong about that perspective. It flatly contradicts the Word of God. He says *"hope maketh not ashamed,"* or as another translation puts it, "hope does not disappoint us" (Romans 5:5).

"Brother Copeland, how in the world can you say hope won't leave us ashamed?" you may ask. "There have been many times when I've hoped and prayed with all my heart and nothing happened. So how can you stand there and tell me hope won't disappoint me?"

I'm not the one who's telling you! I didn't write Romans 5. It was written by the Apostle Paul under the inspiration of the Holy Ghost. So it was God, not I, Who said hope won't disappoint you. And if He said it, it has to be true.

That's why there's no use in you or anybody else whining to me about how it failed you and left you ashamed. I know it didn't. HOPE didn't. If you ended up disappointed, you must have been using something other than hope because God says real, Bible hope won't leave you that way.

"Well, I guess I must not know what real hope is, then!" you say.

That's true. There's a good chance you don't. So maybe we'd better go to the Word of God and find out.

Hebrews 11:1 says, *"Faith is the substance of things hoped for...."*

The first thing we can learn about hope from that scripture is that faith won't do us any good without it. Hope serves as the blueprint for faith. Without it, faith has nothing to do. Hope is the plan that faith carries out. It's the inner image—the picture that the Holy Spirit paints on the inside of you, a picture that's based on the Word of God. Its opposite is despair, which is an image of disaster based on the lies of the devil. Despair says there is no hope.

Did you catch what I said a moment ago about hope being based on the Word of God? That's most important. You may wish that you were two inches taller or that you had a million dollars in the bank. You may even be optimistic enough to think those wishes might come true. But you will not have the hope-that-does-not-disappoint until you go to the Word and find out what God has promised you about those things, and then base your hope on His Word instead of your wishes.

You see, the Bible contains the only workable blueprint for your life (or any other human life for that matter). It's the manufacturer's operating manual. If you ignore the instructions in it, your life simply won't work. It's like putting water in the gas tank of your car. You can do it, but it won't get you anywhere. Your car's operator's handbook will tell you to put water in the radiator and gas in the fuel tank and then it will work. The Word is the manual of life.

Now let's go back to Hebrews 11:1. We've already learned from that scripture that hope must be present for faith to produce. But the reverse is also true. Hope can't produce anything without faith! Faith is the substance.

I remember years ago when I first started studying the subject of faith, I discovered that many people were trying to get by on hope alone, and it wasn't working. They'd say, "We're just hoping and praying," and I'd know right then they wouldn't get anything, because without faith their hope had no substance.

Hope is only the blueprint. You can't take a blueprint all by itself and make a house out of it. You won't be able to live in the thing because it's paper. But if you'll take some substance—lumber and steel and stone—you can follow the blueprint and build a place fit to live in. Faith and hope. Blueprint and building materials. You must have them both.

Remember though, as I said before, the only truly workable blueprint comes from the Word of God. All other blueprints will let you down.

That's why you often hear people say, "Don't get your hopes up." They've had experience with natural hope (hope based on circumstances and human knowledge instead of on the Word of God), and they know that kind of hope will leave you disappointed more often than not.

In Colossians 1:23, Paul warns us not to be moved away from the "hope of the gospel."

That's because any other hope besides "gospel hope" can be spiritually dangerous.

Say, for example, you were dealing with a physical disease and your doctor told you that you only had a small chance of recovering. He'd say that because, based on the natural information he'd have, that might be all he could medically expect—and he wouldn't want to offer you a false hope that might leave you disappointed.

But the Bible says when we operate in the hope of the gospel, we'll not be ashamed. So, instead of clinging to that flimsy thread of limited hope which man has offered you, you'd be much safer going to the Word of God that says, *"By his stripes ye were healed!"* Because those words aren't based on fragmented human information. They're based on the knowledge of God Himself.

Instead of holding onto natural hope, if you built up supernatural hope by meditating on that truth and looking at it night and day, you'd soon have some inner images of strength you could wrap your faith around. You'd even be able to use that supernatural hope to combat the natural evidence around you. Then, instead of having a small hope for recovery, you could have a sure hope for recovery!

Look at Romans 4:18 and you can see what happened when, in the midst of a naturally hopeless situation, Abraham chose to build his life on that kind of supernatural hope. He had received a promise from God that he would become the father of many nations. The problem was, he was already old. So when he turned around and looked at his 90-year-old wife and he looked in the mirror and saw a 100-year-old man, he had no natural hope.

Natural knowledge told him there was no way he could ever have a child. Don't you know that negative knowledge bombarded his thinking? So what did he do? He took the promise of God and the hope of that promise and combated the negative hope coming against him which said, "No way, you can't do it. It's hopeless."

The Bible actually says, *"He hoped against hope."* In other words, he used supernatural hope to overcome natural hope. He locked his mind onto what God said and drove out everything else.

Verse 19 says, *"Being not weak in faith, he considered not his own body now dead... neither yet the deadness of Sarah's womb."*

Now how did he do that? How can you consider not your own body when you're 100 years old and thinking about having a baby? It would be tough, but Abraham was able to do it because *"he staggered not... through unbelief; but was strong in faith, giving glory to God; And being fully persuaded that, what [God] had promised, he was able also to perform"* (verses 20-21). God's promise was at the center of his hope, his faith and his persuasion.

Abraham was fully persuaded. You can be fully persuaded, too. But you can't get that way by sitting around watching television or by spending all your time messing around with the world. You get fully persuaded by purposely meditating on the promise of God until it gets inside you so deeply that no one can get it out.

Another thing that caused Abraham to be fully persuaded was the fact that God changed his name. God stopped calling him Abram and started calling him Abraham, which means "father of a multitude."

If you'll pay attention to this principle, you'll find you can use it in your own life. For example, I learned a long time ago to stop calling myself "poor boy." It didn't matter that on the outside I looked broke. I decided—based on the Word of God—if anyone hollered, "Poor boy!" I wouldn't answer, ever again.

Now, if they were to start hollering for someone who has all his needs met according to God's riches in Christ Jesus, I'd come running. But I decided I wouldn't go by what things looked like anymore. I wouldn't go by what I felt. I had based my life on something bigger than feelings. I had gotten the hope of the gospel inside me.

Abraham called himself "father of a multitude." That was his new name. He wouldn't let anyone call him anything else. People probably thought he'd flipped out. But

Abraham knew what he knew. He was the father of a multitude. He'd seen the blueprint.

Let me give you another example. If I said to you, "Come over here and see my dream house. Man, is it something!" You might say to me, "Where is it?"

I'd answer, "Right here on this piece of paper!"

Then you might tell me, "You don't have any house."

"I certainly do," I'd say. "I just got back from the architect, and you ought to see it. Sit down and I'll show you my house."

Now, that house is real. It started as an image in my mind. Then I described it to the architect and he translated it into symbols and lines. If it hadn't been a picture in my mind and on paper, if I hadn't called it my house, then it would never have been built.

Hope works just like that. People of faith look into the Word of God and they begin to see things. They see things like, *"By his stripes ye were healed."*

I remember the first time I ever saw that particular part of God's blueprint. My mind just wouldn't accept it. If it hadn't been right there in the Bible, I never would have believed it because it was obvious to me I wasn't healed. But the Bible said, *"Ye were healed."* And if *"ye were,"* then I knew I must be.

Once I received that, I started meditating on it. I started building it up on the inside of me. Eventually I was able to see myself healed.

Soon, every time some symptom suggested to me that I wasn't healed, I'd begin to resist it and reject it. You couldn't tell me healing didn't belong to me any more than you could tell me that blueprint wasn't my house. I knew it did. I had a picture of it on the inside of me.

Now I realize there's been some controversy in Christian circles about the right and wrong of visualization. But I can put that argument to rest by assuring you, you are always visualizing something—whether you want to or not. Our minds have been divinely programmed to do that. You have an imagination.

Now we can either use that programming the way God designed it to be used, and live, or we can use it pervertedly, the way Satan has trained us to use it, and die. But we're going to be using it, one way or the other.

Look at the way we talk. Words are simply inner-image transferring devices. When I say, "Dog," I transfer an image from the inside of me to you. You don't sit there thinking, "D-O-G." You see an inner image of a dog. If I say, "Big, black, barking dog," I can modify that image. So when we speak, we're actually exchanging pictures.

As you speak out those inner images, if they are based on the Word of God, faith comes alongside to give them substance. Hope is the blueprint. Faith is the substance. It's a powerful process. How you use it will literally determine your destiny.

There is, however, one thing you need to know: Destiny is not built overnight. It's not what you thought once or twice that got you where you are today. It's what you've thought over and over again. Those inner images are created by repetition, and repetition takes time.

I remember how long it took me to start seeing myself with my needs met according to God's riches in glory by Christ Jesus. The outside of me kept saying I was broke. It said, "You will live in this shack all your life, boy. There's no way you can ever get out of here."

But I started meditating on the Word of God. I practiced thinking about myself God's way. It wasn't easy at first. It felt awkward and unnatural. But that's how you feel when you do something new.

That's how I felt the first time I tried to fly an airplane. During those first few hours, that thing was a monster. When I tried to land it, I hit the nose gear on the ground first and bounced the thing like it was a basketball. Then the next time I landed it, I kept the nose too high and fell several feet, slamming into the ground. I couldn't find the ground. But now, after more than 10,000 hours and 35 years of flying, I don't feel awkward anymore.

That's exactly how you learn to operate in the things of God. You practice. You get into the Word and you meditate on it until the Word begins to change your inner image of yourself and you begin to see yourself with your needs met instead of without. You begin to see yourself in Christ Jesus. You think about it. You talk about it. You start believing in God's promises and acting on them.

"But what if I fail?"

So what if you do! Don't call it a failure. Just get up and go after it again. Learn some more, and learn some more. Work at it. Determine to develop inside you the hope of the gospel.

Just remember, this isn't something that happens in a day or two. It takes time. Before I came to Jesus in 1962, I was one of the most efficient sinners you ever saw. I could sin without even thinking about it. When I got into the things of God and started trying to turn that around, it wasn't easy to do. It didn't take much of anything for Satan to knock me off course.

But over the last 32 years you might say I've had a lot of Holy Ghost flying lessons. I've done a lot of spiritual bouncing and slamming, but I've learned a lot, too. Some of the things Satan used to knock me off balance with years ago won't even get to first base with me now. So be diligent. Stick in there. It will pay off if you don't give up.

The Bible solemnly says, *"Where there is no vision, the people perish"* (Proverbs 29:18). That's how important it is for you to get a grip on God's blueprint for your life.

It's not an option. It's an absolute necessity, because like it or not, your hope, your vision, that inner image inside of you, is determining your destiny—for better, for worse...forever.

## Discovering the Power in Supernatural Expectancy

*Kenneth Copeland*

## Chapter 2

*"Now faith is the substance of things hoped for, the evidence of things not seen."*
— HEBREWS 11:1

Have you ever been in the midst of a faith stand when suddenly it seemed like your faith just quit working?

Maybe you were believing God for healing or financial deliverance or the salvation of your family. Spiritually, everything was in place. You found the scriptures that promised you what you needed. You were firing off confessions of faith like a machine gun.

But as time went by, your spiritual battery began to weaken. The power you had when you first took your stand began to wane, and you developed a gnawing suspicion that nothing would happen.

In desperation, you tried to shove those doubts away by confessing louder and longer. You frantically tried to force your faith to work. But to no avail.

You wound up still sick, still broke, still surrounded by unsaved relatives...and wondering what went wrong.

In the end, you probably just chalked it up as a faith failure.

But I'm about to tell you something that will change your life if you'll pay attention to it. It certainly changed mine. It's this: *What you experienced was not the failure of your faith...it was a breakdown of your hope.*

## Faith...or Desperation?

Most believers don't pay much attention to hope. They don't think of it as very important. They certainly don't consider it to be as important as faith. But the fact is, faith won't function without hope.

That's because *"Faith is the substance of things hoped for"* (Hebrews 11:1). Sometimes

I say it this way, "Hope is the blueprint of faith." When hope is lost, faith loses its aim. It no longer has a mission to accomplish. It just scatters uselessly in every direction.

I remember one time in particular some years ago, when that happened to me. At God's instruction, I had given my airplane to another preacher and then ordered another to replace it. During the weeks while the new plane was being manufactured, I began to believe God for the full amount I needed to pay for it.

I hooked up my faith to the promises of God and I was going along fine for awhile. But just a few days before the plane was scheduled to be delivered to me, I realized I was $20,000 short.

As the delivery date grew closer, I became more and more alarmed. I started making faith confessions as fast as I could. I'd say, "Thank God, I have that $20,000. In Jesus' Name, I-have-it-I-have-it-I-have-it-I-have-it."

But the problem was, I was no longer confessing in faith, I was confessing out of desperation.

I knew something had to change, so I gathered up my Bible and my tapes, got in my boat, and went out to the middle of the lake to spend some time with the Lord. But when I got out there, I was still saying, "Thank God, I have that $20,000. In Jesus' Name, I-have-it-I-have-it-I-have-it-I-have-it."

Suddenly, the Lord spoke up on the inside of me: *KENNETH, BE QUIET!* He said, *I'm tired of hearing that. Just hush and let Me show you what I can do.*

When He said that, something happened inside me. My hope came alive again. Suddenly I was expectant instead of desperate. I started eagerly anticipating what God was about to do, instead of fearing what would happen if He didn't come through in this situation.

Sure enough, the $20,000 I needed for that airplane came in and the pilot who delivered it to me ended up getting saved and filled with the Holy Spirit in the process.

But none of that would have happened if I hadn't pulled aside, locked myself away with the Word for several hours, and let the Spirit of God rebuild and rekindle the hope inside me.

## Supernatural Expectancy

Before you can understand how important hope is, you have to realize that real, Bible hope is not "wishing." That's worldly hope. People in the world say, "I sure wish I would get a raise at work," when what they mean is, "I want a raise. I don't think I will get it...but it would be nice if I did."

The kind of hope the Word of God talks about is much stronger than that because it's not based on wishing or wanting. It is based on your covenant with God and the anointing God has provided to carry out that covenant in your life.

In fact, Ephesians 2:12 says before you knew Jesus, you were *"without Christ [or without the anointing], being aliens from the commonwealth of Israel, and strangers from the covenants of promise, having no hope, and without God in the world."*

"But Brother Copeland," you say, "I'm a believer. I know God's promises. Doesn't that mean I have all the hope I need?"

Not necessarily. You see, hope comes when you take those promises, keep them before your eyes and in your ears until they begin to build an image inside you. Hope comes when you begin to see yourself *with* what God has promised you—instead of seeing yourself *without* it.

When you have hope, you have a supernatural expectancy that what God has promised will come to pass in your life.

The Apostle Paul talks about that kind of supernatural expectancy in Philippians 1:19-20 where he says, *"I know that this shall turn to my salvation through your prayer, and the supply of the Spirit of Jesus Christ, According to my earnest expectation and my hope, that in nothing I shall be ashamed."*

In that scripture, Paul uses two different words from the Greek language, each of which can be translated *hope*. One of them means "the happy anticipation of good." The other can be defined as "eager longing, strained expectancy, watching with an out-stretched head, and abstraction from anything else that might engage the attention."

When divine hope comes alive in you, you're so locked in on the Word of God, you can't be distracted from it. I know what that's like. There have been times in my life when I was so focused on something God had called me to do, and I was so tuned in to what the Word said about it, I couldn't think about anything else.

People would try to have a conversation with me and I'd always end up talking about my hope. It would come up so big inside me that at those times, I was bigger on the inside than I was on the outside.

When your hope gets that strong, it doesn't matter what kind of unbelief the devil tries to throw your way, it just bounces off you. You're so one-track minded, you can't be drawn off course.

Back when Gloria and I first found out about faith, I was like that all the time. If someone walked up to me and said something that sounded like unbelief, I would just explode all over them! (I'm still like that, actually, I've just learned to be a little more gentle about it.)

One night I was in a bookstore in a church where I was preaching when such an explosion took place. I had stepped up to the cash register to buy my book and when I reached in my pocket to get my money, I sniffed.

I just sniffed! I don't know why I did it. I guess I just felt like sniffing. When I did, the lady running the bookstore said to me, "Is it a cold or hay fever?"

Almost before I knew what I was doing, I had opened my mouth and started spurting the Word as fast as I could talk. "THE WORD OF THE LIVING GOD SAYS IN GALATIANS 3:13, I'M REDEEMED FROM THE CURSE OF THE LAW. DEUTERONOMY 28:61 SAYS ALL SICKNESS AND DISEASE ARE UNDER THE CURSE AND I AM REDEEMED FROM

THE CURSE OF HAY FEVER. I DON'T HAVE COLDS, IN JESUS' NAME! I'VE BEEN WASHED IN THE BLOOD OF JESUS! AND BY JESUS' STRIPES I AM HEALED! HE BORE MY SICKNESSES AND CARRIED MY DISEASES...."

I nearly pinned that lady to the wall with the Word of God. Finally, she exclaimed, "Forgive me, Brother Copeland. I knew I was in trouble when I said that! But I finally understand what you've been preaching about. I've had migraine headaches all my life. I have one right now, but if you'll lay your hand on me, I'll be healed."

I did—and she was!

What happened to her? That explosion of the Word went into her heart and suddenly she could see herself healed. Her hope came to a crisp sharpness. She saw an inner image of who she is in Christ Jesus and that no migraine could stay in her body. The minute she did, the force of faith went to work and brought that image to pass!

That's what the Bible means when it says *"faith is the substance of things hoped for"*!

## Stick Your Neck Out

How do you develop that kind of hope? You stay in the Word until your neck stretches out. I particularly like that part of the definition of hope because I know what it means to have your neck stretched.

When I was a little boy, my grandfather was my hero. He was a full-blooded Cherokee Indian and I wanted to act like him, look like him, curse like him, chew tobacco like him and spit like him—much to my mother's chagrin. When my mother would tell me that he and my grandmother were coming to see us, I would get so excited I could hardly wait.

Every minute or two, I'd run to the window to see if they had arrived. Every noise sent me running for the door. I tell you, my neck was stretched out in anticipation. My Pawpaw was coming and I expected him any moment.

That may sound like a silly example, but the Lord once told me if people would just expect Him to move as much as a child expects his grandparents to arrive, He could move on their situation and change things drastically by the power of His Spirit.

That's what happened in Acts 3 to the crippled man at the gate Beautiful. He had been sitting by that gate begging, his head down and his eyes to the ground. But when Peter and John walked by and said, "Look on us!" that man lifted his head and began to expect.

Hope rose up in him because he was *"expecting to receive something of them"* (verse 5).

Of course, he received a lot more than he was expecting—he expected alms, but he got legs! That's because his expectancy hooked into their expectancy—and, believe me, their expectancy was running high!

It hadn't been more than a few days since Jesus had risen from the dead, defeated the devil and all of hell with him. It hadn't been but a few days since Jesus had looked the disciples straight in the eyes and said, "Now, you go into all the world and use My Name to cast out devils. You lay hands on the sick and they'll recover" (see Mark 16:15-18).

I can just imagine Peter saying, "Hey, John, you know that crippled beggar down there by the temple? Come on, let's go use the Name on him!"

They could see themselves doing what Jesus said they could do. Their hope was "white hot." So they went charging down to the temple and said to that cripple, *"In the Name of Jesus Christ of Nazareth rise up and walk."*

When they said it, they grabbed him. He had to walk, brother! They yanked him completely off the ground (Acts 3:1-8).

What made them do such a thing? Expectancy!

They didn't tiptoe up to that gate, look around to make sure no one was watching and then whisper, "Dear Lord, if it be Thy will, heal this poor crippled man."

The only people who pray "if it be Thy will" are those who don't have any hope or expectancy. If you've been praying that way, stop it! Go to the Word and find out what God's will is. The Word of God is His will. It is His will for you to be well. It is His will for you to be prosperous. It is His will for you to lay hands on the sick and it is His will for them to recover.

So stay in the Word until you're so confident and expectant that your neck is stuck out in anticipation. Meditate on the Word until your hope gets crisp and that image inside you gets strong and clear.

Stay in there until you're so full of expectancy that when someone walks up to you and says, "Good morning," you jump on them like a chicken on a bug saying, "Yes! Bless God! It is a good morning. Do you have anything wrong with you? I'll lay hands on you right now and you'll get healed!"

Once hope gets that strong, it becomes courage...and hope plus courage equals the spirit of faith in action!

## The Spirit of Faith

The Apostle Paul refers to the spirit of faith in 2 Corinthians 4:13 saying, *"We having the same spirit of faith, according as it is written, I believed, and therefore have I spoken; we also believe, and therefore speak."*

The spirit of faith speaks! It calls things that be not as though they were. It makes faith confessions—not because it's "supposed to" or out of desperation, but because it's so full of eager anticipation and confident expectation it can't keep its mouth shut!

The spirit of faith says, "I don't care what God has to do, He'll turn the world upside down if He has to, but He will change this situation for me."

Every time I talk about the spirit of faith, I think about my high school football team. For years, the teams from that school had been losing teams. But something happened to the bunch on my team. A spirit of winning got into them.

When we were sophomores, we were on the B squad. We were the nothings. But somehow we got the idea that we could win. Every year the B squad would have to scrimmage the varsity team, and usually the varsity just beat the daylights out of the sophomores.

But the year our B squad played them, that changed. We didn't just beat them, we had them down by several touchdowns, just daring them to get the ball, when the coach called off the game. He was so mad at the varsity team, he didn't even let us finish.

What happened to that little B squad? We reached the point where we expected to win. We had an inner image of ourselves as winners, and it eventually took the best team in the state to beat us.

The same thing happened to Gloria and me in 1967 when we went into the ministry. We began to have an inner image of preaching the Word of God to thousands upon thousands of people. It was 10 years before we could gather up more than a handful of them at a time for one service, but we didn't let that stop us.

We saw the thousands in our heart and in our mind and we just kept our necks stuck out—in more ways than one— expecting God to bring the people. Sure enough, He did.

Of course, there were some hard times. Times when people stayed away from our meetings by the millions. Times when I preached to 17 people with the same intensity that I would preach to 6,000.

That's what hope does. It keeps you intensely focused on God's promise. It keeps you seeing that promise on the inside, even when you can't see it on the outside. It keeps you operating by the spirit of faith.

When you have hope, the devil can't beat you down. He can't tear you down. He can't stop your faith from working. Everyone around you can just stop in their tracks, but you'll keep right on going.

When the devil knocks you down, you just get up with a deeper resolve to hit him harder the next time...and harder the next time...and harder the next time.

You get to the point where you expect God to move with such vigor that all the distractions in the world can't turn your head. All the failures of the past drift into nothingness. You can't even remember them anymore because you're so absorbed with the expectation of what God is about to do.

When that happens, you no longer sit around wondering what went wrong. You blast off into the glory of God, laying hold of His promises and watching your dreams come true. You live the kind of life that those who give up hope will never know.

# Good News!

## Chapter 3

*"God was in Christ, reconciling the world unto himself, not imputing their trespasses unto them; and hath committed unto us the word of reconciliation."*
— 2 CORINTHIANS 5:19

Happy
Caldwell

"Go ye therefore and teach all nations that God is mad at them."

That's not what Jesus said in the Great Commission. But all too often, that is the message traditional religion has preached.

People (believers and unbelievers alike) have been told how unworthy they are. They've been told what sorry creatures they are. They've been told they don't act right or talk right or pray right.

Sound familiar? If so, I have some good news for you today: God is not mad at you. In fact, He's not mad at anybody!

The Bible says He [God] *"was in Christ, reconciling the world unto himself, not imputing their trespasses unto them"* (2 Corinthians 5:19). Every person ever born on this earth has already been guaranteed by God the right to stand before Him without any sense of guilt or shame. Every person, no matter how covered in sin he may be, qualifies to receive God's righteousness. Not everyone takes advantage of it, but everyone has the opportunity.

Statements like that shock religious people. Do you know why? Because, as Romans 10:3 says, *"They being ignorant of God's righteousness, and going about to establish their own righteousness, have not submitted themselves unto the righteousness of God."*

That's what religion always does. It tries to establish its own righteousness, its own rules, its own right-standing with God. Religion says, if you act right, talk right, dress right and look right, then God will give you favor.

But God isn't religious. He says, *I don't want you to establish your own righteousness. I want to give you Mine. But before you can receive it, you have to quit trying to establish your own.*

You can't earn the righteousness of God. There's nothing you can do to deserve it. It's God's gift. All you can do is receive it.

When I accepted Jesus Christ as my Lord, God declared me righteous. I didn't look very righteous. I called on liquor stores back then. Alcohol was my business. I sold it and I drank it. But the day I submitted to Jesus, my life changed.

I went back to work the next Monday morning in those same liquor stores. I didn't know a thing about the Bible. I only knew I was different. Soon, I began to tell people that I had two kinds of spirits, alcoholic spirits and the Holy Spirit. "Which one do you want to hear about first?" I'd ask.

I found that many of them were interested in Jesus. They weren't interested in religion, but they were interested in knowing that God was no longer *"imputing their trespasses"* to them. They were interested in knowing that He had settled the account of the whole world's sins. That was good news!

The sad thing is many believers—people who have already been made righteous in

Jesus—don't fully grasp that news. They don't realize God isn't mad at them. They don't realize they can go boldly before the throne of God without shame—dressed in the righteousness of Jesus Christ.

That's because they've been taught to focus more on how they've messed up than on what Jesus has done for them. They're more sin-conscious than they are righteousness-conscious.

One of the first steps to becoming righteousness-conscious is to learn the difference between having your sins forgiven, and having your sins remitted. Remitted is a word that should never be used in connection with a believer because a man's sin is remitted only once.

When sin is remitted, at the moment of salvation, the Word tells us we become *"a new creature: old things are passed away; behold, all things are become new"* (2 Corinthians 5:17).

You see, the problem we had before we were saved was not all those little individual sins we committed. They were only the symptoms. The problem was the condition of our heart. The problem was our sin nature. No matter how hard we tried to be good and act right, that nature kept us imprisoned in sin.

But when we made Jesus the Lord of our lives, our sin nature died and a righteous nature was born in us. Sin no longer had dominion over us. Righteousness set us free!

That kind of freedom wasn't available to people in Old Testament days. Back then, before the blood of Jesus had been shed, there was a "reckoned righteousness" with God, gained through the blood of sacrificed bulls and goats. Those sacrifices covered the individual sins, but they didn't change the hearts of people. People kept on committing the same sins every year because their nature was still the nature of sin.

*"For it is not possible that the blood of bulls and of goats should take away sins"* (Hebrews 10:4). But what the blood of bulls and goats could not do, Jesus' blood did. *"...This man, after he had offered one sacrifice for sins for ever, sat down on the right hand of God...For by one offering he*

47

*hath perfected for ever them that are sanctified"* (verses 12, 14).

How long will Jesus' sacrifice for sin last? Forever. You are forever righteous through the blood of Jesus.

I know you still miss it and sin sometimes. But even when you do, it's not the same because your heart is different. God doesn't see you the same way He did before you were born again.

Think of it this way. If you're a parent, you may know your child has done something wrong, but as far as you're concerned, he's still your child and he's wonderful. He may need to be corrected, but there's nothing wrong with him. You know he wants to please you. He just needs more training so he can learn to do things right.

Do your children fall out of good standing with you just because they mess up? Certainly not. It's the same way in the family of God. Once you've been born again, your nature is changed. You don't want to sin even when you do.

And when you do sin, you have Someone on your side. *"...If any man sin, we have an advocate with the Father, Jesus Christ the righteous"* (1 John 2:1). *"If we confess our sins, [God] is faithful and just to forgive us our sins, and to cleanse us from all unrighteousness"* (1 John 1:9).

While remission changes your nature, forgiveness erases your mistakes. And that's the final word on sin. God has taken care of the sin problem forever. When Jesus became sin and put sin away, the sin problem became a closed issue with God.

You can still sin if you choose. God won't stop you. The Holy Spirit will deal with you if you'll listen...but if you won't, you can do what you will. But you don't *have* to sin. You don't have a sin nature anymore. You have a righteous nature.

God *"hath delivered us from the power of darkness, and hath translated us into the kingdom of his dear Son"* (Colossians 1:13). You've been translated out of one kingdom and into another one.

People are so worried about the devil. They're fighting the devil and bombarding the gates of hell all over the place. But I like what one author wrote: "If you really understand your righteousness in Christ and your authority as a believer, you will pay no attention to the devil. You'll just go on and do your job."

Jesus said, *"I beheld Satan as lightning fall from heaven. Behold, I give unto you power to tread on serpents and scorpions, and over all the power of the enemy: and nothing shall by any means hurt you"* (Luke 10:18-19).

Satan has no authority over you unless you give it to him. Jesus has stripped him of all authority and placed it in your hands. As He said in the Great Commission, *"All power is given unto me in heaven and in earth. Go ye therefore..."* (Matthew 28:18-19).

That's good news, Church! Let's tell it!

# The Forgotten Power of Hope

## Chapter 4

*"...God is able to make all grace abound toward you; that ye, always having all sufficiency in all things, may abound to every good work."*
— 2 CORINTHIANS 9:8

*Kenneth Copeland*

I want you to look with me at a word most people think they understand. It's a word you've heard thousands of times, in church and out. A word you've used yourself over and over again—probably without having the foggiest notion what it really means.

I'm talking about the word *hope*.

"Oh, Brother Copeland, I know what the word *hope* means!"

No, you don't. Not unless you've studied it in the Word of God. Because in today's language the word *hope* has lost its meaning. It doesn't even resemble the hope spoken about in the Bible.

For example, these days you might hear someone say, "I sure do hope Joe is coming for dinner." What does that mean? It means, "I don't know if Joe is coming for dinner, but I sure wish he would." In that context, the word hope is the same as the word wish. It carries with it an element of doubt.

But real Bible hope isn't like that at all. In fact, it's just the opposite. If you look up the Greek definition of the word *hope,* you'll find it means "to be intensely expectant, to be confidently looking forward to something you fully expect to happen."

You can see this kind of hope in action in Philippians 1:19-20. There, the Apostle Paul says, *"I know that this shall turn to my salvation through your prayer, and the supply of the Spirit of Jesus Christ, According to my earnest expectation and my hope..."* For emphasis, Paul used the two Greek words there that mean earnest expectation. In other words, he was saying to them, "This thing is so inevitable I'm just burning up with expectancy!"

Most believers don't know anything about that kind of burning-up-with-expectancy hope. They just know about the wishing kind of hope. You ask them, "Will you get your healing?"

"Oh, I hope so...," they answer. Then they just go on and on expecting to be sick—and of course they are—and never understand why.

Wishing won't accomplish anything in the kingdom of God. But hoping will, especially when you couple it with faith and love! First Corinthians 13:13 says, *"And now abideth faith, hope, charity [or love], these three...."* That puts hope in some very powerful company! It is one of the three most powerful elements in the universe. It is one of the three eternal and living substances that run the entire kingdom of God.

I preach a lot about faith. I'm constantly teaching believers that they can't get anything done in the kingdom of God without faith. But do you want to know something? Faith can't get anything done without hope—intense expectation!

Hebrews 11:1 says, *"Now faith is the substance of things hoped for...."* In natural terms you might say faith is the building material and hope is the blueprint. You have to have hope before faith can begin building anything in your life.

Now when I say you need to have hope, I'm not saying you just need to start thinking optimistically. Positive thinking is fine and it certainly is better than negative thinking. But just thinking optimistically will never cause you to burn up with confident expectancy like the Apostle Paul did. Positive thinking will never give you Bible hope.

Real Bible hope has to be based on God's Word. Otherwise, it has no foundation under it.

For instance, someone who has liver cancer might say to me, "I fully expect to be healed of this liver condition." I might say to them, "What makes you believe that when the doctor just declared your condition incurable?"

Now, that person can respond in one of two ways. He can tell me he believes he'll be healed just because he wants it to be true. If he does, he has no foundation beneath him. He's just wishing. That's the world's kind of hope, but it definitely isn't the Bible kind.

If he has Bible hope, he'll say, "I will be delivered from this liver condition because God's Word says every sickness and every disease is under the curse of the law, and Galatians 3:13 says Jesus has redeemed us from the curse of the law, being made a curse for us. In other words, Jesus has already redeemed me from the curse of this liver condition. That's why I fully expect to be delivered from it."

When you have that kind of clear, Word-based image inside you, you have real Bible hope—and it's an absolute must for anyone who wants to live by faith. Without that kind of hope, your faith has nothing to grab onto and you'll let the devil talk you out of your healing (or whatever else you need to receive from God). He'll look you right in the face and say, "Well now, I don't see any healing taking place in your body. It looks to me like you're as sick as you've ever been. Obviously, this healing business just isn't working for you."

The devil will feed those kinds of words into your mind and try to get you to think about them. If you do, you'll be in trouble. But if you'll dwell on the Word of God until the hope of the gospel rises up on the inside of you...if you'll meditate on God's promises until you begin to have an inner image of yourself healed and strong...if you'll speak those promises day after day...you'll be able to look at the devil and say, "Oh, shut up! I know what I know and I know God's Word is working for me. That Word says I'm healed and that's what I'm looking at and nothing else."

I don't mind telling you, it's rarely easy to do that. (If it were easy, everybody would be doing it!) Sometimes you have to get rough on yourself to make yourself stand on the Word of God when you're in great physical pain. Your emotions will want to take over. They'll push you to start crying and feeling sorry for yourself.

But don't do it. Instead, take charge of those emotions by the Spirit of God within you. Don't ever let your emotions cause you to back away from hope. If you do, you'll kill it.

Yes, I said you'll kill it. You see, hope is a living thing. Paul says hope "abides." To abide means to live. Only living things abide, so hope is a living thing and you have to guard it and nourish it with the Word of God. You have to feed it with the Word so it can grow.

If you'll do that, hope will paint a picture on the inside of you, a picture of God's promise fulfilled in your life. It will give you an inner image of yourself healed and prosperous, with your loved ones saved, your marriage restored or whatever else you've been hoping for. Hope will paint that picture so clearly inside you and make it so real, you'll begin to be blind to what you see on the outside.

Let me give you an example: You've prayed for your son or daughter to be set free from a drug habit. You can get such a clear picture of what that child will be like after he has been delivered that he starts looking great to you now—even though he still may be giving you trouble!

You'll actually get to the point where you won't see what a louse he or she is being right now because you've seen him in Jesus with the eyes of your spirit. People will say, "I don't know what she sees in that child." They won't understand that you're looking at him through eyes filled with hope.

If you'll continue to look at him that way and not let the devil shake you, if you'll refuse to jump up in that child's face and tell him what a sorry old thing he is, one of these days that child of yours will look on the outside just like you see him on the inside. He'll be delivered!

No doubt about it, that kind of hope is strong spiritual stuff! Where do you go to get it?

You go to the same place you go to get faith—the Word of God. You bathe your brain in that Word every day. You think about it all the time, wherever you are and whatever you are doing.

You keep your faith tapes going. You keep someone preaching to you all the time.

Because as you keep feeding your spirit on God's Word, hope will begin to rise up. God's pictures will start to develop in your spirit. You'll begin to see them on the inside of you. In fact, they'll get bigger inside you than the circumstances around you.

Then, when the devil comes and tries to show you an image of some beat-up, run-down person wearing your name, you'll just send him packing. You'll shake your head and say, "No sir, that's not a picture of me. This is a picture of me..." and you'll start talking the Word of God!

As you meditate on those inner pictures hope has painted with God's Word, you'll begin to believe you are what the Word of God says you are. You'll begin to realize you're not what the world says you are. You're not what your parents or your friends say you are. You're not even what you think you are. You are what GOD says you are! You're the righteousness of God in Christ Jesus (2 Corinthians 5:21)!

When the devil comes at you with his junk, you'll reach in, get out that picture hope has given you, and put it in front of your eyes. You'll say, "Devil, I'm not looking at you. That sick, poverty-stricken, failure-bound person you're describing isn't me. This is me. I'm the fellow with the healed body. I'm the fellow with all my needs met according to God's riches in glory. I'm the fellow who is more than a conqueror in Jesus!"

Power pictures. That's what hope produces. Inner pictures faith can build on. But you need to understand, these are not Polaroid™ 60-second snapshots. The development of hope takes time.

For instance, when I discovered healing, I didn't have any trouble with that. I could easily see that if God made a body, He could certainly fix it. That seemed obvious. But I had a difficult time seeing how God could ever fix my financial problems. I couldn't see the prosperity picture clearly at all.

But the more I studied the Word and meditated on it, the more my thinking changed. Hope began to develop. I grabbed hold of 2 Corinthians 9:8 that says, *"God is able to make all grace abound toward you;*

*that ye, always having all sufficiency in all things, may abound to every good work."*

An inner image of all my needs being met with plenty left over for every good work began to grow by God's Word. I began to see it on the inside. I got a revelation of it.

After that it wasn't a matter of how God would meet my financial needs. It was a matter of fact that He'd already met them. All I needed to do was get in line with Him.

After a while, that revelation was so real in my consciousness that I began to think like a man without debt. I began to talk like a man without debt.

It wasn't long until Gloria and I were totally, completely debt free. We didn't owe anybody anything and God was the One Who had done it. We hadn't asked anybody for a dollar.

I've never written an appeal letter in this ministry and I never will because I don't have to. My needs aren't met by your giving. My needs are met by my giving because I'm standing on the Word that says, *"Give and it shall be given unto you again."* That's why my needs are met. God is my source, so I don't have to put any pressure on you. Now, God may use your giving to meet my need, but that's not where my earnest expectation is built. My hope is built on the forever Word of God's promises.

I learned how to think that way by studying Jesus. He never looked to people to meet His need. It's a good thing, too. One time when He was preaching, everyone in His congregation walked out. They just got up and left. The only people who stayed were the members of His own staff.

Did He get upset about it? No, He just went right on to the next place and held another meeting. That time He had a landslide. But the landslide didn't affect Him any more than the walkout because those people weren't His source. God was His source. He was there to help them. He didn't call them there to help Him. They did help Him, but not because He pressured them to.

Do you get the picture? I did. Twenty-plus years ago, it came alive inside me. I took hold of it and it changed my financial life forever.

I got a picture of prosperity from God's Word, and faith made that picture a reality. That's how the process always works. First you have to have the hope, then faith goes into action. Hope is the inner image that your faith becomes the substance of. Hope is the blueprint. Faith is the material.

Faith can't build on wishes. How many times have you heard someone say, "I sure do wish God would do something for me"? The rest of the statement hangs unspoken in the air, "...but He probably won't."

That's not faith. That's unbelief. But it works the same way faith works—only backward. Fear is actually faith in the negative dimension. It's faith in failure, danger or harm. When someone is meditating on negative thoughts or, "worrying," as we call it, he or she is developing inner pictures. Not pictures of hope, but pictures of despair.

Just as fear is the flip side of faith, despair is the flip side of hope. It's an inner image of failure, sickness, poverty or whatever else the devil wants to inject into you. Despair is actually hope in the negative and fear, like faith, brings it to pass.

Do you see how powerful this process is? This is the process that controls the course of your life. These inner images, whether they be of hope or despair, become the blueprint for your faith or fear, and ultimately control your destiny.

Once you understand that, you hold the key to your future. You hold the key to becoming everything God wants you to be. It doesn't matter where you are right now. You may be sick. You may be broke. You may be defeated. It doesn't matter!

What you must do is dig into the Word and begin building your hope. Start developing God's pictures within you. As long as you have an image of your own defeat on the inside of you, you're destined to be defeated on the outside as well. But change that inner image with the Word of God and no demon in hell will be able to hold you down.

Jesus came to change the inner man. *"If ye continue in my word,"* He told us, *"then*

*are ye my disciples indeed; And ye shall
know the truth, and the truth shall make
you free"* (John 8:31-32).

Get that truth working inside you. Put
it in there until hope begins to paint new
pictures in your heart. Then hang onto
those pictures relentlessly. Don't ever let
them go. Eventually—inevitably—faith will
make those pictures as real on the outside
as they are on the inside.

*"For as he [a man] thinketh in his heart,
so is he"* (Proverbs 23:7). It's the pictures
inside you that determine your destiny. Get
yourself some power pictures. God's Word
is full of them. The question is, are you?

# The Anointing Factor

## Chapter 5

*"Wherefore remember, that ye being in time past Gentiles in the flesh...were without Christ [the Anointed One], being aliens from the commonwealth of Israel, and strangers from the covenants of promise, having no hope, and without God in the world: But now in Jesus [the Anointed One] ye who sometimes were far off are made nigh by the blood of Christ [the Anointed One]."*
— EPHESIANS 2:11-13

Kenneth
Copeland

In May of 1993, hopelessness hit the headlines. It grabbed the attention of the nation as it drove angry, violent crowds into a destructive rage on the streets of east Los Angeles.

Businesses were burned. Stores looted. Innocent bystanders were injured and even killed as people who felt trapped by circumstances, condemned to poverty and powerless over their own futures, erupted in frustration.

As the startling scenes reached into living rooms across this country by television, people began to ask, "What can we do? These people are hopeless! How can we change this situation?"

Some answered by calling for more government programs. Others cried out for financial aid. Still others called for more educational and employment opportunities.

But I can show you by the Word of God that none of those things by themselves would have solved the situation. They wouldn't have gone to the source of the problem. In Ephesians 2:11-12, the Lord reveals what that source is. Describing the condition all of us were in before we were born again, He says: *"Wherefore remember, that ye being in time past Gentiles in the flesh...were without Christ, being aliens from the commonwealth of Israel, and strangers from the covenants of promise, having no hope, and without God in the world."*

According to the Word of God, hopelessness isn't caused by lack of money. It isn't caused by lack of education. It isn't caused by negative circumstances. Hopelessness comes from being without God in the world. It comes from being a stranger to His covenant.

Anybody anywhere can have hope if they know Jesus and the covenant promises of God. Your background, race, or financial status doesn't matter. You can live in the worst ghetto in the world and still have hope in God because He isn't limited by man's resources. He isn't limited by man's prejudices. God is an equal opportunity employer!

Some people have said to me, "You ought not preach that prosperity message in poverty-stricken areas. You'll get those people's hopes up, and they don't have the same opportunity to prosper that you do."

Yes they do!

I've seen God prosper people in places where there was absolutely nothing. No food. No jobs. No welfare program. Nothing! There is one country in Africa where the government wanted a tribe to die out so they just stopped the flow of food and began to starve them to death. But that plan failed because some Holy Ghost-filled African Christians refused to give up hope.

They knew their covenant, so they prayed "give us this day our daily bread." Do you know what happened? The people got fed and the government went under!

## More Than Wishful Thinking

Understand this, though. When I say hope, I'm not talking about the weak, wishful-thinking kind of attitude most people call hope. Real, Bible hope isn't a wish. Hebrews 11:1 says, *"Faith is the substance of things hoped for...."* There's no room for faith in wishing! For example, take the statement, "I sure do wish God would bless me financially." There's no place in that statement for faith. It just won't plug in anywhere.

The Apostle Paul said in Philippians 1:20, *"According to my earnest expectation and my hope, that in nothing I shall be ashamed...."* If you'll look up the two Greek words translated earnest expectation and hope, you'll find they're two different words that both mean the same thing. So hope is earnest expectation.

There's plenty of room for faith in earnest expectation. Say, for instance, "I earnestly expect to receive financial blessings. I earnestly expect to be free from poverty." Faith can plug right into that statement. It just follows naturally. Faith becomes the substance of that statement.

Someone might ask, "How can you so intensely expect to prosper when the unemployment rate is up and the economy is down?" You can answer, "What I'm earnestly expecting isn't dependent on the world's economy. It's based on what God has promised in His covenant. Because He said it, I earnestly expect it!"

Can you hear the faith in those words? Certainly! Real, Bible hope just opens the door so faith can walk right in!

Why don't we see more of that kind of hope in the Body of Christ? Because it is born out of the promises of God's covenant. And most Christians are using their believing faculties to believe some sort of religious system that men have designed instead of believing the Word of God. Despite the fact that they're born again with the seed of

71

hope inside them, baptized in the Holy Spirit and walking around with a Bible tucked under their arm, they've become strangers to the covenants of promise.

You can tell those folks that 2 Corinthians 8:9 says Jesus became poor so we might be rich and they'll answer, "Oh, yes, amen. I know it says that, brother. But I just don't know whether to take the Bible literally or not."

The reason they don't know whether or not to take the Bible literally is because they're not spending any time in the Word as a covenant. That's what the word *testament* means. Did you know that? The New Testament is the new covenant! It's not some kind of religious book. It is God's will and testament written down. It is a covenant of promise. It is God's blood-sworn oath.

I want you to imagine for a moment that you made a blood covenant with someone. You both cut your wrists, bound your hands together, mixed your blood and swore an oath to each other in your own blood. That would be serious, wouldn't it?

You know it would! But you have a covenant even more serious than that with Almighty God. It's a covenant ratified not by the tainted blood of a sinful man, but by the sinless blood of Jesus.

I've meditated on that fact until it's real to me. So when I pick up the New Testament, I'm not just reading a history book. I'm reading a copy of God's will and testament and in my mind, I have Jesus by the hand and His blood is flowing down my wrist. Once you get a revelation like that, hope is no problem!

## Figure in the Anointing

With those things in mind, let's go back to Ephesians 2 and dig a little deeper into what God is telling us about hope: *"For we are (God's) workmanship, created in Christ Jesus unto good works, which God hath before ordained that we should walk in them"* (verse 10).

Before we read any further, I want you to stop for a moment and notice the phrase *"created in Christ Jesus."* To truly understand that phrase, you need to realize that the word *Christ* is a Greek word. Why the English translators failed to translate it, I don't know. But that failure has cost us a great revelation.

You see, the word *Christ* isn't Jesus' last name. It's not a title. It's a word with a very significant meaning. *Christ* actually means *anointed*. To *anoint* is literally "to pour on, smear all over, or rub into." So the Anointing of God is to have God poured on, smeared all over, and rubbed into.

Some time ago, the Spirit of God further clarified that definition for me. He said, *The Anointing of God is God on flesh doing those things only God can do.*

Practically speaking, what does that Anointing of God on flesh do for us? According to Isaiah 10:27, it destroys the yoke of bondage.

Some people say the anointing breaks the yoke. But the word used in Isaiah isn't *break,* it is *destroy.* It literally means to obliterate so completely that there is no evidence the yoke ever even existed.

Now, let's go back and read Ephesians 2, translating the word Christ: *"Wherefore remember, that ye being in time past Gentiles in the flesh...were without [the Anointed One], being aliens from the commonwealth of Israel, and strangers from the covenants of promise, having no hope, and without God in the world: But now in [the Anointed] Jesus ye who sometimes were far off are made nigh by the blood of [the Anointed One]"* (verses 11-13).

According to those scriptures, before you were born again, you were without the Anointed One. Well, if you were without the Anointed One, you were also without the anointing, right? But now, you are in the Anointing of Jesus. That anointing is available to you in every situation to destroy (obliterate completely!) every yoke of bondage.

That's why you can have hope in the most hopeless situations. It doesn't matter who you are or what color your skin is. It doesn't matter if you never made it past the sixth grade. You can break out of that hopeless situation if you'll factor in the anointing.

The anointing factor is what the world always forgets. They say, "We'll build this wall so big nobody will ever get through it. We'll build it big enough to block out the gospel and keep the people under our thumb." But they fail to figure in the anointing factor. It will destroy that wall. If you don't believe it, ask the believers in Berlin!

I strongly suggest you begin factoring in the anointing in your life from this moment forward. If someone says, "Well, brother, you can't expect to succeed. You can't expect to prosper. You can't expect to get healed," ask yourself, "Is there a yoke holding me back?" If the answer is yes, then rejoice because the anointing will destroy it!

"But Brother Copeland, I can't ever expect to get a good job because I can't read."

Is that your yoke? Then, believe God and He'll destroy it.

I know a fellow who hadn't gone to school at all. God taught him how to read the Bible, but for a long time he couldn't read anything else. One day, he walked into the principal's office in the local high school and said, "I want to earn my diploma."

The principal looked across his desk at this 40-year-old man and said, "OK, we can probably work something out. How much schooling have you had?"

"None," the man answered.

Shaking his head, the principal told him there just wasn't any way to overcome that kind of obstacle. But the man was persistent. "Now wait a minute," he said. "The Lord Jesus Christ has let me know that if I do my part and you do your part, He'll do His part. Yes, sir. There is a way."

Sure enough, in less than a year he had his high school diploma.

## Don't Be a Stranger

Nothing is too big a problem when you figure in the anointing! So take hold of that anointing by beginning to expect. Start expecting something good to happen to you. Lay hold of the hope that's set before you in the promises of God.

Don't be a stranger to those promises. Dig into them, find out what God has said about your situation. Then start saying, "I expect it because God promised it!"

Think about that promise and meditate on it. Let it build an image inside you until you can see yourself well...until you can see yourself with your bills paid...until you can see yourself blessed and prosperous in every way.

If you'll do that, you'll eventually get bigger on the inside than you are on the outside. Your hope will grow so strong that the devil himself won't be able to beat it out of you.

Most believers never experience that kind of confident hope because they allow their emotions to pull them off course. They don't feel healed or they don't feel blessed, so they let the promises slip.

You can avoid that pitfall by anchoring your soul. Anchor it by becoming a follower of people like Abraham *who through faith and patience inherit the promises.* (See Hebrews 6:11-20.)

The Bible says Abraham hoped against hope (Romans 4:18). He used the hope of the promise of God to fight against the natural "hope" (or hopelessness) that told him it would be impossible for Sarah and him to have a child.

Romans 4:21 says he was *"fully persuaded that, what (God) had promised, he was able also to perform."* Now, Abraham wasn't always fully persuaded. There was a time after God had promised to give him a child when he asked, "How can I know these things will happen?"

God answered him by cutting a covenant with him. Abraham killed the covenant sacrifice animals, split them down the center, laid the halves opposite each other and God walked in the blood of those animals. I believe with all my heart Abraham saw God's footprint in that blood.

From then on, Abraham's soul was anchored. His mind couldn't argue with him. His emotions couldn't argue with him. His old, dead body couldn't argue with him. His barren wife couldn't argue with him. That covenant put an end to all arguments. From then on, Abraham was fully persuaded. Fully expectant.

## Anchor Your Soul

God has made a covenant with you just as surely as He made it with Abraham. But instead of making it in the blood and body of animals, He made it with the broken body and shed blood of His own Son— Jesus the Anointed One. That's what should be on your mind when you take communion. Hebrews 6:17-19 says:

> **Wherein God, willing more abundantly to show unto the heirs of promise the immutability of his counsel, confirmed it by an oath: That by two immutable (unchangeable) things (the body and the blood of Jesus), in which it was impossible for God to lie, we might have a strong consolation, who have fled for refuge to lay hold upon the hope set before us: Which hope we have as an anchor of the soul, both sure and stedfast....**

Friend, we have hope because we're in blood covenant with Almighty God! Through Jesus we have access to Him. We *"are no more strangers and foreigners, but fellow-citizens with the saints, and of the house-hold of God"* (Ephesians 2:18-19)!

When we're confronted by impossible situations in this world, we have a covenant right to factor in Jesus! Factor in the power of His Word! Factor in His Anointing!

Some say, "That sounds too easy." No, it's not easy! When the devil begins to pull the noose of hopelessness around your neck with poverty or sickness or some other terrible situation, you have to fight and fight hard. Not by burning buildings and robbing stores—but by grabbing hold of the hope in the Word and using it to demolish every thought that would rise up against it.

*"Casting down imaginations, and every high thing that exalteth itself against the knowledge of God, and bringing into captivity every thought to the obedience of Christ"* (2 Corinthians 10:5).

The battleground where hope is won or lost is not on the streets, it's in the mind. It's in the imagination where expectancy begins to take form. So take your stand on that battleground. Begin now to expect the anointing to destroy the yokes in your life. Begin now to expect God to keep His covenant promises to you.

Fight for that expectancy in the Name of Jesus. Take your hope, fill it with faith and storm the gates of hell. They will not prevail against you!

# Renewing Your Mind

## Chapter 6

*"But we all, with open face beholding as in a glass the glory of the Lord, are changed into the same image from glory to glory, even as by the Spirit of the Lord."*
— 2 CORINTHIANS 3:18

Gloria
Copeland

Christianity is not just another religion. It is the life of God abiding within and flowing out of the believer. Other religions leave you the same person you were before. But the wonderful thing about the Christian life is that it will completely transform you.

When you are born again, your spirit is instantly transformed into the image of God. The spirit is the part of you that takes on the nature of God. According to the Word, once that happens you should immediately start the process of changing your soul. The Bible calls it "renewing the mind."

Your soul is your mind, will and emotions. Spiritual growth is determined by how much your soul is changed by the Word of God. The more you know the Word, the more you conform to the image of Jesus. When you are born again, nothing is wrong with your spirit—the life of God is in there—but you are hindered from living a spiritual life by a soul (mind) that thinks like the world instead of like God.

After becoming a Christian, the Bible instructs you to *"put on the new man, which after God is created in righteousness and true holiness"* (Ephesians 4:24). This means that your soul and body are to take on the same image that is in your spirit. This happens through the process of changing your mind, your will and your emotions to understand and walk in the ways of God. We are to conform to the image of God's Son (Romans 8:29). You and I ought to act just like Jesus. The only thing that stands in the way is our soul. Without a renewed mind, we could not dare to walk and act like Jesus.

That's why Romans 12:2 tells us *"be ye transformed by the renewing of your mind."* The word *transformed* is translated from the Greek word from which we get the term *metamorphosis*. This Greek word is used in the Scripture in two other places.

One such account is when Jesus was transfigured on the Mount. The other is in 2 Corinthians 3:18: *"But we all, with open face beholding as in a glass the glory of the Lord, are changed into the same image from glory to glory, even as by the Spirit of the Lord."* *Changed* is the same word in the Greek as *transformed* and *transfigured*. Our souls are changed when we spend time beholding the Lord in the Word and in prayer. It is a natural process like metamorphosis.

Renewing our minds causes our outer being to be transformed in much the same way as a caterpillar is changed into a butterfly. As we behold Him, our outer man changes to match the inner man which is created in righteousness and true holiness.

The world would have you think that God is a liar. Yet God tells you that Satan is the liar, and in between these two adversaries is your soul. Here is where the spiritual battle is fought. Therefore, your soul must be anchored. Anchored to what? To the Word. To eternal things. If it is moored to this world, you will never walk in victory or in the power of God. If your soul is not fixed on eternal things, it will not hold steady in the time of crisis.

When you become a Christian, you are sustained from the inside. Your spirit is steady in adversity. You are upheld and maintained by your spirit man and not by your intellect or reasoning. *"For the word of God is quick, and powerful, and sharper than any twoedged sword, piercing even to the dividing asunder of soul and spirit, and of the joints and marrow, and is a discerner of the thoughts and intents of the heart"* (Hebrews 4:12).

God's Word divides (distinguishes between) the soul and the spirit. Nothing else can cause you to recognize whether you are being led by your soul and natural thinking or whether you are following your spirit which is led by the Holy Spirit.

Every problem, weakness or difficulty you have could be solved immediately if you could know the mind of God. But it takes effort, dedication and faithfulness to renew your mind. Mind renewal is not like the new birth. It is a process and doesn't come overnight. Though your spirit is renewed and transformed, your soul must be saved. Saved from what? From the world's influence and thinking.

James 1:21 is quite clear concerning this: *"Wherefore lay apart all filthiness and superfluity of naughtiness, and receive with meekness the engrafted word, which is able to save your souls."* You can't just read the Word. It must be implanted in your soul (your mind) and be received with meekness.

Meekness is often misunderstood. It is a thing of power, not weakness. It is an attitude in which we accept God's dealing with us as good. Therefore, we do not resist His correction or guidance. Meekness is giving your will to God and letting Him change it. So, your soul is saved as you yield your will to God's will.

The Scripture says that God energizes and creates in us the power and the desire to will and to work for His good pleasure

(Philippians 2:13). He works from the inside out, not from the outside in. He takes the image of the Word that is in our spirit and grafts it into our soul as we behold Him. Only then can we outwardly express the image of Jesus that we inwardly possess.

But this takes conscious effort. If you are just going to give God a couple of hours a week, your mind will not be renewed. The Word won't be implanted in you. You might know it with your head, but it's the engrafted Word in your soul that changes you. It's the Word of God that controls your thinking and transforms your life.

So, take the time to get away from the world and study God's Word. Meditate on it, and let it change you from the inside out. *"Draw nigh to God, and He will draw nigh to you"* (James 4:8). Make a conscious effort to allow the Word of God to be engrafted into you. Only then will you begin to understand His Word and His will. Only then will you be on your way to renewing your mind.

# More Than You Can Dream

*"...hope maketh not ashamed; because the love of God is shed abroad in our hearts by the Holy Ghost which is given unto us."*
— ROMANS 5:5

*Kenneth Copeland*

These days, when I say the Word of God can heal your body, pay off your debts and bring you victory in every area of your life, not everyone believes me. Most wouldn't admit it outright, but it's true nonetheless.

They don't intentionally doubt the Word, of course. They're just so overwhelmed by the problems in their own lives, they're not sure anything (natural or supernatural) can help.

When they see Gloria and me so blessed and prosperous, they think, *Sure, it's easy for you to live by faith. You have a great life. But what can God do with a life as messed up as mine?*

If you ever struggle with that question, let me tell you. God can do for you exceedingly, abundantly above all that you can ask or think. After more than 25 years of ministry, I can say that, not only because it's the Word of God, but also because it's a living reality for me.

You see, I wasn't always blessed. When I first learned about faith, I was a failure looking for somewhere to happen. I wasn't just scraping the bottom of the barrel, I was underneath with the barrel on top of me! Then one day I was reading Deuteronomy 28 and I saw all the blessings God's people are supposed to have in their lives.

To be quite honest, I got mad. *Where are all these blessings that are supposed to belong to me?* I thought. As far as I could see, I didn't have even one of them. Yet the Bible clearly said:

> ...all these blessings shall come on thee, and overtake thee, if thou shalt hearken unto the voice of the Lord thy God. Blessed shalt thou be in the city, and blessed shalt thou be in the field. (I wasn't blessed anyplace!)

**Blessed shall be the fruit of thy body....** (My children kept getting sick so they weren't very blessed, either.) **Blessed shalt thou be when thou comest in, and blessed shalt thou be when thou goest out.** (I wasn't.)

**The Lord shall cause thine enemies that rise up against thee to be smitten before thy face: they shall come out against thee one way, and flee before thee seven ways.**

**The Lord shall command the blessing upon thee in thy storehouses, and in all that thou settest thine hand unto; and he shall bless thee in the land which the Lord thy God giveth thee (Deuteronomy 28:2-4;6-8).**

I didn't have any land. I didn't have any storehouse. In fact, I'd heard that God wouldn't bless you with a storehouse at all because He didn't want you to have anything.

**And the Lord shall make thee plenteous in goods, in the fruit of thy body, and in the fruit of thy cattle, and in the fruit of thy ground,**

in the land which the Lord sware unto thy fathers to give thee. The Lord shall open unto thee his good treasure, the heaven to give the rain unto thy land in his season, and to bless all the work of thine hand: and thou shalt lend unto many nations, and thou shalt not borrow (verses 11-12).

I don't mind telling you, that looked good to me. All I'd ever known how to do was borrow, and I had even depended on borrowed money all my adult life.

## From Galatians to the Garage

Religion might have tried to explain the absence of those blessings in my life by telling me God made those promises to the Israelite nation, not to me. But I had already found out from Galatians 3:29 that everything God promised Abraham belongs to the gentiles now through Christ Jesus. For *"if ye be Christ's, then are ye Abraham's seed, and heirs according to the promise."*

No, there was no doubt in my mind that these blessings were legally mine. The only question I had was, "How can I get my hands on them?"

As I dug into the Word, I found the answer. To enjoy the blessings of Abraham, I was going to have to walk in the same kind of faith he did.

Now, as in Abraham's day, faith opens the door to God's promises. To me, that was good news.

Not everyone sees it that way, however. Some people want the blessings without having to walk by faith. But like it or not, that's just not the way things work.

"Well," you say, "I wish they did!"

No, you really don't. God didn't set up the system of faith and prayer in order to make things difficult for you. He did it because Satan and his crew are always trying to steal our blessings. God's system is designed to keep them from pilfering our inheritance.

That's not hard to understand. After all, we protect things of value, even in the natural world. Think about how your bank works, for example. You have money deposited there. You know it belongs to you. But if you want to receive it, there are some things you have to do.

Why is that? It's certainly not to keep you from getting your own money—it's to keep other people from getting it. The procedures are for your benefit.

Of course, if you want to, you can ignore the procedures. You can go into the bank and squall and cry, beg, plead and jump up and down, but if you don't follow the established procedures, you won't get your money.

In that same way, God's promises belong to you. They're locked up in the spiritual treasure house of Almighty God. To access them, you'll have to take the time to learn the procedures. You'll have to study God's Word and discover His ways.

My willingness and even eagerness to do that was about all I had going for me back there in those early days, but it was enough. I was so desperate to learn faith that I locked myself in my garage with some tapes of Kenneth E. Hagin's messages about our inheritance in Christ Jesus.

For a week, I didn't talk to anyone else; I didn't listen to anyone else. I just went out there with the garbage, my Bible and my tape recorder. I told Gloria, "Don't call me more than once for a meal. If I don't show up in five minutes, go ahead and eat without me. I'll come in and sleep when I'm ready and then I'm coming right back out here. If anybody calls me, I'm not available."

I stayed out there with those tapes hour after hour. I couldn't get enough of the Word of God.

I'm the same way today. I can't get enough of it. I don't care what else is going on in the world, I'm going to stick with the Word. It brought me out of debt. It healed me. It healed my children. It has taken me through everything that has ever come my way, and I'm not about to turn loose of it now.

## Build a Dream

Let me make it clear though, I didn't get a new set of circumstances overnight.

When I walked out of the garage at the end of that week, my debts were just as big and my problems just as real as when I began. But something inside me had begun to change.

Hope had been born in me.

When I say "hope," I don't mean the weak "I wish" kind of hope the world gives. I mean the Bible kind of confident expectancy that comes when you get an inner image of something that hasn't happened yet. That kind of hope, Romans 5:5 says, never disappoints you.

Most people aren't familiar with godly hope. They are, however, quite experienced in "worry," which is a negative form of it. Worry begins with a thought in someone's mind. As it progresses, that thought becomes a mental picture.

Once the picture is formed, every time the person thinks of that thing, he can see it happening. As he concentrates on that picture, mulling it over again and again, it gets stronger and clearer.

What he's actually doing is meditating on something that hasn't come to pass yet.

Eventually, he'll begin to talk like it has already happened because of the inner image he has built inside his consciousness. If he talks it long enough, that image will show up as a reality in his world.

Hope works that same way. The difference is, hope's pictures are not based on natural circumstances and devil-inspired fears, but on the Word of God.

If you're going to follow the faith of Abraham, you need to practice developing that kind of hope.

"But, Brother Copeland, I told you before, my situation is hopeless!"

It's probably not any more hopeless than mine was—and it certainly is not any more hopeless than Abraham's was. When God told him he was going to have a son, he was already 100 years old. Obviously there was no natural hope for that to happen. To make matters worse, his wife, Sarah, was in her 90s and had been barren all her life.

Yet the Bible says Abraham hoped against hope (Romans 4:18). He built a picture in his mind because of God's promise to him, a picture that was contrary to the pictures of childlessness that his circumstances had given him.

Abraham drew hope from what God had said to him and hung onto it. He drew it into his spirit and imagined having a son. He built it into his consciousness until he drove out every other idea.

It doesn't matter how far down you are today—financially, physically or any other way—you can do the same thing. You can begin to build dreams out of God's Word. A good foundation for them is Deuteronomy 28. It's God's Word and I can tell you from experience, it is good dream-building material.

God intended for man to be a dreamer. He built into us the capacity to do it. But He didn't intend for us to be limited by natural thoughts and circumstances. He meant for us to dream beyond them.

That's what Abraham did. He locked into God's dream—and it was bigger than anything he could have thought up on his own.

It will be that way for you too. God's dream is bigger than your dream for yourself.

It is, as I said before, exceedingly, abundantly beyond all you can ask or think! (See Ephesians 3:20.)

## What Are You Becoming?

Once you get that dream inside you, things will begin to change. No, all your problems won't disappear overnight any more than mine did. But you'll respond to them differently. When they rise up in front of you and threaten to defeat you, God's dream will stir in your heart.

You'll start saying, "Wait just a minute. I'm the head, not the tail. I'm blessed, not cursed. I don't have to put up with this mess. I happen to be a child of the King Himself. He sets my table in the presence of my enemies. No weapon formed against me can prosper!" (See Deuteronomy 28:13, Psalm 23:5 and Isaiah 54:17.)

Once you start dreaming from the Word of God, you'll start acting on those dreams and your faith will bring them to pass.

That's what Dr. David Yonggi Cho did in Korea. He was a dying man, riddled with tuberculosis, when he came into the kingdom of God and started studying God's Word. He didn't have any religious people around him to tell him not to dream. He just took his Bible and started building dreams in his heart—things he wanted to do for God, for his nation, for his people.

He dreamed of building the biggest church in the world. He dreamed of sending missionaries all over the world. Today, that dream is a reality.

Dr. Cho pastors a church in Seoul, Korea, with over 700,000 members. Although the nation had no money when the church started, his church is able to send out millions of dollars a year to the foreign mission field.

Just think, all that started with one man dreaming by the Word of God. Like Abraham, he hoped against hope. He wrapped his faith around the supernatural picture painted by the Word of God, instead of the impossibilities painted by the world.

Look at Romans 4:18 again. It says Abraham *"believed in hope,* (notice the next phrase) *that he might become..."*

What are you becoming? Abraham was 100 years old and still planning what he would become. He still had his eye of faith focused on something he couldn't attain on his own. Something that couldn't come to pass without the supernatural power of God. He set out to become the father of many nations at 100 years old.

You know, when you get right down to it, it doesn't really matter much what you've been in the past. It doesn't matter whether you've left a colossal mess behind you or 25 years of ministry—what matters is what you're becoming today.

The Apostle Paul put it this way: *"...this one thing I do, forgetting those things which are behind, and reaching forth unto those things which are before, I press toward the mark for the prize of the high calling of God in Christ Jesus"* (Philippians 3:13-14).

## Better Than Good

If you're not sure what you're becoming, let me give you a hint. You're going to become whatever you think about and talk about all the time.

I can listen to you talk for 30 minutes and tell you exactly what you're going to become. It doesn't take a prophet to do that. It just takes someone who will listen to your words.

So, listen to yourself. If you don't like what you hear, change it. Become someone better by beginning to think God's Word, talk God's Word and act on God's Word.

Nobody on earth can determine what you're going to become but you. Yes, you! Don't blame it on the devil. He can't change it. Don't blame it on your parents, your background or your circumstances.

Forget those things which are behind... and do what Abraham did. The Bible says *"he considered not his own body now dead, when he was about an hundred years old, neither yet the deadness of Sarah's womb..."* (Romans 4:19). He just said to himself, "Old man, you don't count. Neither do you, Granny. What counts is

God's Word, and I am exactly who God says I am."

Do you want to become who God says you are? Do you want to be healed? Do you want to become free financially? Do you want to become a powerful witness in your neighborhood?

What is your dream? You can have it if you'll learn to live by faith.

If you don't have a dream yet, get one. Fill your heart full of the Word of God. Let Him show you what's possible. Trade your negative, natural hope for the supernatural promises of Almighty God and learn to "hope against hope."

I can tell you, your life will really be good when you're living Matthew, Mark, Luke and John instead of the 6 o'clock news. No, it will be better than good—it will be miraculous.

So miraculous, in fact, that sometimes when you tell people the Word of God will heal them, prosper them and set them free, they'll look at your life and say, "Sure it's easy for you to live by faith. You have a great life. But what can God do with a life as messed up as mine?"

Then you'll just smile and say, "Friend, God can do more for you than you'll ever dream. I can tell you that from experience. You see, I wasn't always this blessed...."

# You Are a Candidate for a Miracle

## Chapter 8

Jesse Duplantis

*"...be thou strong and very coura-geous, that thou mayest observe to do according to all the law, which Moses my servant commanded thee: turn not from it to the right hand or to the left, that thou mayest prosper whithersoever thou goest. This book of the law shall not depart out of thy mouth; but thou shalt meditate therein day and night, that thou mayest observe to do according to all that is written therein: for then thou shalt make thy way prosperous, and then thou shalt have good success. Have not I commanded thee? Be strong and of a good courage; be not afraid, neither be thou dismayed: for the* LORD *thy God is with thee whither-soever thou goest."*

— JOSHUA 1:7-9

If you're facing an impossible situation today, if you can't see a way out and you're so discouraged you're ready to quit, I have seven words for you that can change everything. Seven words that can— if you'll dare to believe them—turn total defeat into the most glorious opportunity for victory you've ever known: You are a candidate for a miracle.

That's right. If you're in Christ today (Notice I said "in Christ" not "in church." These days there are a lot of people in church who aren't in Christ.), you should be expecting God to do the impossible for you.

You should be running for a miracle today the same way a political candidate runs for office. But with one big difference. You don't have to be voted in to get your miracle. You just have to enter the race— because your miracle has already been won!

Every challenge you face today was overcome by Jesus 2,000 years ago when He went to the cross. He paid the price to heal every sickness or disease that may be in your body. Because of Jesus, there's an answer that's older than any problem you now have.

If you have cancer, you're a candidate for a miracle.

If you have diabetes, high blood pressure, heart trouble (or whatever!), you're a candidate for a miracle.

If you're financially broke, you are a candidate for a miracle.

If you're looking for someone to marry, you're a candidate for a miracle.

No matter what kind of need you may have today, you're a candidate for a miracle!

## Problems, Get Out of My Face!

The first chapter of Joshua tells us about one particular man who was a candidate for a miracle. His associate, Moses, had just died and Joshua was facing the task of taking 5 million notoriously rebellious Israelites into the Promised Land.

God said to him, *Now, Joshua, here's the situation.* "Moses my servant is dead; now therefore arise, go over this Jordan, thou, and all this people, unto the land which I do give to them, even to the children of Israel" (verse 2).

Notice that God didn't tell Joshua about all the trouble he was going to meet when he got over there. He didn't tell him about the wall at Jericho. He didn't tell him there would be fierce giants to defeat.

He just said, "Arise and go, Joshua. You're a candidate for a miracle."

Then He said, *If you'll get up and go...*

**Every place that the sole of your foot shall tread upon, that have I given unto you, as I said unto Moses. From the wilderness and this Lebanon even unto the great river, the river Euphrates, all the land of the Hittites, and unto the great sea toward the going down of the sun, shall be your coast. There shall not any man be able to stand before thee all the days of thy life: as I was with Moses, so I will be with thee: I will not fail thee, nor forsake thee (verses 3-5).**

Look again at that last verse. Notice God didn't say that no one could stand against Joshua during this "Promised Land

Campaign" he was about to begin. He said, "All the days of your life, Boy, nobody will be able to get in your face and knock you down" (my paraphrase, of course).

God told Joshua he'd be a candidate for a miracle all his life. That's good news, isn't it?

"Yeah, Brother Jesse, but that promise was for Joshua, not you and me."

God is no respecter of persons! God didn't love Joshua any more than He loves us. So if we'll do what God told him to do, no one will be able to stand before us either.

## Forward...or Back?

What exactly did God instruct Joshua to do?

> ...be thou strong and very courageous, that thou mayest observe to do according to all the law, which Moses my servant commanded thee: turn not from it to the right hand or to the left, that thou mayest prosper whithersoever

**thou goest. This book of the law shall not depart out of thy mouth; but thou shalt meditate therein day and night, that thou mayest observe to do according to all that is written therein: for then thou shalt make thy way prosperous, and then thou shalt have good success. Have not I commanded thee? Be strong and of a good courage; be not afraid, neither be thou dismayed: for the Lord thy God is with thee whithersoever thou goest (verses 7-9).**

Just like Joshua, if you meditate on the Word of God, if you believe it and obey it, you're a candidate for a miracle today. You may feel like you're in the desert, but you're standing on the boundary of the Promised Land.

The only question is: Will you go forward...or will you turn back?

The devil is going to try to convince you to turn back. He's going to work to distract you from the Word of God and scare you into settling for a nice life in the desert.

But listen to me. You may build 100 churches in the desert. You may draw water out of the Jordan, cultivate the dry land and think you've found heaven. But you'll be mistaken. Don't live in the desert in a church with a cultivated yard! You'll be outside of the will of God. He wants you in the Promised Land.

"But, Brother Jesse, it would take a miracle to get me past all these problems I have and into the Promised Land."

No problem! You're a candidate for a miracle!

*Well, then,* you may wonder, *why am I having such a hard time receiving one?* Because you remember too well that fallen state you were in before God saved you.

Most all Christians have that problem. That's why they have difficulty believing God will work a miracle for them. They believe, for instance, that God will heal... but they're not sure He will heal them!

But it's time we change that kind of thinking. We need to quit dwelling on that old, fallen state and focus instead on the

fact that God has made us His righteousness in Christ Jesus! We are in Him!

Sometimes I speak so boldly, it makes
people mad. They say, "Who do you think
you are?!" I ask them, "How much time do
you have? It would take me a long time to
tell you who I am because I'd have to tell
you everything Jesus is. I'm in Him!"

## Hey Everybody, Watch This!

Because of that attitude, when a big
obstacle arises in my life, the first thing I
say is, "Well, it's miracle time. It's time to
grow. It's time to get in the Word of God."

I had to learn that early in my ministry
because I faced some situations where a
miracle was the only thing that was going
to get me through.

I'll never forget one particular time, just
after my brother-in-law, Jules, was saved. He
was a very successful lawyer and through
Cathy's and my witness, he had come to the
knowledge of Jesus Christ. Of course, we'd
told him about the healing power and

promises of God and—as baby Christians usually do—he just believed without question and said, "Wow! That's great!"

I was getting ready to preach a meeting one night when my brother-in-law called me. He said a woman had come into his office who had been in an accident in the restaurant where she worked. She had been paralyzed as a result of it and wanted to sue the restaurant.

Jules said, "Well, lady, you have two choices. We can take the legal route and get you a lot of money...or you can go with me to my brother-in-law Jesse's meeting tonight and get healed. Which do you want?"

She said, "Well, I guess I'll go to the meeting."

So Jules called me and said, "Jesse, I'm bringing this paralyzed woman tonight and I've told her she'll get healed. That's right, isn't it?"

I assured him that was right and then after I hung up, I said, "God, what are we going to do?" You see, I had a problem because I had seen some people get healed and some not.

*We're at the Promised Land, Jess,* God answered. *Are we going to walk across or are we going to drag this paralyzed woman back to the desert and bury her?*

That night I preached as long as I could. (I was hoping she might get tired and go home.) Finally, I couldn't put it off any longer and I said, "All right, it's time for God to heal."

When Jules brought the woman up front, I determined to pray for her as quietly as possible so as not to attract any attention. But Jules had other ideas.

"HEY, EVERYBODY!" He called out. "WATCH! GOD'S GOING TO HEAL THIS WOMAN. OK, Jesse, now do it."

That woman was a candidate for a miracle—and so was I! I tried to make things easier by closing my eyes while I prayed for her but the Lord said, *Open your eyes.*

"No!" I answered.

*Open your eyes, Jesse!*

So I opened my eyes, told the woman God was going to heal her and then prayed with every fiber of my being. All of a sudden—wham!—both her hands went up in the air, she was knocked down by the power of the Holy Ghost, and was totally, miraculously healed!

You may think that's an unusual incident. And, to some it might be. But you and I serve an unusual God, and we should expect the unusual to be "the usual" in our lives.

Why? Because we are candidates for a miracle.

I want to burn that phrase into your mind. I want it to so mark your thinking that any time you have trouble from now on, instead of slipping automatically into despair, you'll follow the instructions God gave to Joshua. You'll get into the Word of God and not turn from it to the left or to the right. You'll go to bed reading it. You'll get up reading it. You'll meditate on it until you digest all the nutrients in it and it fills you with the power of God.

You'll say boldly, "No, I'm not giving up, praise God. I'm going on. I'm stepping into the Promised Land because I'm a candidate for a miracle!"

# Turn Your Hurts Into Harvests

*"...my God shall supply all your need according to his riches in glory by Christ Jesus."*
— PHILIPPIANS 4:19

Kenneth Copeland

What do you do when someone mistreats you?

I didn't ask what you want to do. I didn't ask what your automatic fleshly reaction is. I already know that.

Your natural, knee-jerk response is the same as mine. You want to strike back. You want to do something or say something that will even the score. If you can't manage that, you might settle for a few hours (or days or years) of feeling sorry for yourself. You might try to ease your wounded feelings by telling someone how wrongly you've been treated.

On a purely natural, human level that's how we all want to react when someone does us wrong. But I want to tell you something today. If you're a born-again child of the living God, you have no business just reacting to things on a natural, human level.

God has called and equipped you to live on a higher level. He's given you the power to respond in a supernatural way when someone does you wrong. He's given you the power to respond in love.

"Oh, Brother Copeland, that's too hard. I don't want to do that!"

Yes, you do—and here's why. If you will train yourself to respond God's way, you can take mistreatment and transform it from the curse the devil intends it to be into a seed of tremendous blessing in your life.

When you learn to obey God in the face of persecution, you can literally get rich—in the areas of finances, favor and opportunity—off the very persecution the devil sent to keep you down.

## Serious Business

Make no mistake, that is the devil's intention. He sends people across your path to offend you and mistreat you for the express purpose of stealing the Word of God—and the anointing that goes with it—out of your life. Mark 4:17 says, *"...persecution ariseth for the word's sake...."*

The devil knows how powerful you are when you are anointed. He knows because he once was anointed himself. The Bible says before evil was found in him, he was the "anointed cherub." So it is his one ambition to trick you into cutting yourself off from that anointing.

That's why he sends bigots to insult you and thieves to steal from you. That's why, whenever he can, he goads people around you into being insensitive and unappreciative. He wants you to get offended and cut off your supernatural power supply.

Most believers don't realize it, but that's what offenses do. You can see that in Matthew 11:4-6. There, the disciples of John the Baptist came to Jesus and asked if He was truly the Anointed One. Jesus answered and said to them: *"Go and show John again those things which ye do hear and see: The blind receive their sight, and the lame walk, the lepers are cleansed, and the deaf hear, the dead are raised up, and the poor have the gospel preached to them. And blessed is he, whosoever shall not be offended in me."*

We need to realize, my friend, that offenses are serious business. They are sent by the devil to rob us of the anointing and block the flow of the blessings of God. That fact alone should be enough to make us decide never, ever, to be offended again.

I know I've made that decision. I've determined that no matter how someone may insult my intelligence, my beliefs or even my race, I'm not willing to lose my anointing over it.

No matter how they treat me, or what they might call me, I will not take offense.

Now I realize someone may be reading this and thinking, *Yeah, that's easy for you to say! Nobody says and does the things to you like they do to me!*

That may be true. Although I am an Indian, and have had ample opportunity for offense, where race is concerned, I know there are many people who have suffered much more mistreatment than I have. But I can say this: No matter what color you are, you are welcome in more churches than I am. I've had entire books written for the express purpose of criticizing me. How many books have they written about you?

I only bring those things to your attention because I want you to know that dealing with offenses isn't any easier for me than it is for anyone else. I've come up against some hard people and some hard situations in my life. So I know if God can see me through, He can do the same for you.

## Rejoice!...No Kidding

Once we decide we will take a devil-sent opportunity for offense and turn it into a harvest of blessing, the first thing we need to know is what God wants us to do in that situation. If we're not supposed to strike back, if we're not supposed to get our feelings hurt and go off in a huff, what are we supposed to do?

First Peter 4 answers that question: *"Beloved, think it not strange concerning the fiery trial which is to try you, as though some strange thing happened unto you: But rejoice, inasmuch as ye are partakers of Christ's sufferings; that, when his glory shall be revealed, ye may be glad also with exceeding joy. If ye be reproached for the name of Christ, happy are ye; for the spirit of glory and of God resteth upon you..."* (verses 12-14).

God doesn't want us to cry and complain when someone does us wrong. He doesn't want us to sue them. He wants us to REJOICE!

I can just hear your old flesh groan: "Man, you have to be kidding! I'm supposed to rejoice when someone does me wrong? What do I have to rejoice about?"

Plenty!

According to Jesus, persecution sets you up for blessing. It opens you up for great rewards! Jesus made that very clear in Luke 6. He said, *"Blessed are ye, when men shall hate you, and when they shall separate you from their company, and shall reproach you, and cast out your name as evil, for the Son of man's sake. Rejoice ye in that day, and leap for joy: for, behold, your reward is great in heaven"* (verses 22-23).

To get the full meaning of what Jesus was saying there, you have to realize what the word *blessed* means. It's not just a weak, religious sentiment. To be God-blessed means you're empowered by Almighty God Himself to prosper and succeed. It means you're empowered by the Holy Spirit to be exceedingly happy with life and joy in spite of any outside circumstances.

Think about that for a moment. When people mistreat you, they're actually giving you the opportunity to receive greater measures of power and success from the Spirit of God. They are opening the door for you to step up to a higher plane of heavenly reward!

Religion has taught us that we couldn't enjoy such heavenly rewards until after we die. But nothing could be further from the truth. God intends for us to make use of our heavenly rewards here on this earth where we need them!

123

You see, as believers, we each have a heavenly account that functions much like a natural bank account. The Apostle Paul refers to that account in his letter to his Philippian partners. He commended his partners for giving to him, not because he wanted gifts from them, but because he desired fruit that would abound to their account.

Paul's partners had made deposits in that heavenly account through their giving, so he was able to boldly say, *"...my God shall supply all your need according to his riches in glory by Christ Jesus"* (Philippians 4:19).

Jesus also spoke of that heavenly account when He said, *"Lay not up for yourselves treasures upon earth, where moth and rust doth corrupt, and where thieves break through and steal: But lay up for yourselves treasures in heaven, where neither moth nor rust doth corrupt, and where thieves do not break through nor steal: For where your treasure is, there will your heart be also"* (Matthew 6:19-21).

If you've studied the Word under this ministry any length of time, I'm sure you already know how to lay up treasure in your heavenly account by giving financially into the work of God. You know about the spiritual law of seedtime and harvest. You know that when you give to God of your material resources, He multiplies it and gives it back to you a hundredfold (Mark 10:30).

But let me ask you this: Did you know you can do the same thing with persecution? Did you know that you can plant it as a seed by obeying God, by leaping and rejoicing in it instead of taking offense?

Sure you can! And when you do, it will bring forth a harvest of blessing!

What's more, because persecution attacks your soul and the very Anointing of God on your life—which is far more precious than anything money could buy—the value of the harvest it brings is absolutely priceless. The seed of persecution when planted according to the Word will be worth far more to you than any financial seed you could ever plant!

Now, I'll be honest. It's a tough seed to sow. You have to sow it out of commitment.

It doesn't feel good to do it. But the harvest is worth the pain.

I know that not only from my own experience, but from watching the experience of others. For instance, one friend of mine has refused to take offense at the bigotry directed against him because of the color of his skin. He has so succeeded in blessing and loving the white people who have persecuted him that now some black people are mad at him. "He doesn't even know he's black anymore!," they'll say.

But my friend doesn't take offense at them either. He just prays for them and goes right on gathering up his harvest. It's quite a harvest, too! That man has favor everywhere he goes. He's invited to places few people get to go. He's blessed financially beyond most people's wildest dreams.

The man is getting rich off racism!

## It's Worth More as a Seed

Someone might say, "Well, that sounds good! I wonder if it would work like that for me?"

It will if you'll put it to work. Look back at that passage in Luke 6:27 where Jesus explains this principle and says, *"I say unto you which hear...."* In other words, this will work for anyone who will listen. All you have to do is hear it and do it.

> Love your enemies, do good to them which hate you, Bless them that curse you, and pray for them which despitefully use you. And unto him that smiteth thee on the one cheek offer also the other; and him that taketh away thy cloak forbid not to take thy coat also. Give to every man that asketh of thee; and of him that taketh away thy goods ask them not again...But love ye your enemies, and do good, and lend, hoping for nothing again; and your reward shall be great, and ye shall be the children of the Highest: for he is kind unto the unthankful and to the evil. Be ye therefore merciful, as your Father also is merciful.
>
> Judge not, and ye shall not be judged: condemn not, and ye shall

not be condemned: forgive, and ye shall be forgiven: Give, and it shall be given unto you; good measure, pressed down, and shaken together, and running over, shall men give into your bosom. For with the same measure that ye mete withal it shall be measured to you again (verses 27-30, 35-38).

For the most part, we've misunderstood what Jesus was saying about turning the other cheek and giving to the guy who tries to steal from us. We thought He was saying we should just lie down and let people run over us. But that wasn't His point at all!

He was trying to teach us about this seedtime, harvest principle. He was trying to show us how to get blessed. He was saying, "Don't sue the person who stole your shirt and try to get your shirt back. Give it to him. Then give him your coat too. Those things will be worth more to you as seeds than they would be if you kept them. If you'll sow them instead of fighting to keep them, the power of God will go to work on your behalf. He'll multiply that seed and bless you with a hundred times as much!" If you fight, you do it on your own. If you give, all of heaven will get in the situation with you.

I'll never forget the first time God was able to get the truth of that principle through to me. It was years ago when Gloria and I were on our way to preach a meeting in San Francisco. I was walking through the airport with a little Minolta camera hanging over my shoulder. Back then, that was the ministry camera and Gloria was the ministry photographer. So that camera was important to us.

I had walked around that airport for a while when suddenly I realized my camera was gone. Someone had stolen it right off my shoulder! To put it very mildly, I was irritated.

I started looking around the airport for the thief. I thought, *If I find you, you turkey, I am going to whip you good!*

But right in the middle of my upset, the Spirit of God interrupted my thinking. *If you take that attitude,* He said, *you'll lose that camera!*

"What are you talking about, Lord?" I answered. "I've already lost it!"

*No, it isn't gone yet.*

I'd learned from Oral Roberts about the seed, plant, harvest principle, so I caught on to what the Lord was telling me in a flash. I said, "Lord, I see it!" Then I turned to Gloria and said, "Listen, let's agree on this. I'm giving that camera to whoever took it off my shoulder. I'm sowing it as a seed into that person's life and I'm praying that God will use it to get him saved. I'm believing that every time he touches that camera, the Anointing of God will come on him and draw him to Jesus. Even if the police catch the thief with the camera in his hand, I will say, 'Don't charge that man with any crime. I have given him that camera.'"

Of course, Gloria agreed and we boarded the plane to San Francisco. After we got settled in our seats, I started talking to the Lord about the seed I'd planted. I said, "Lord, I know that camera had value and we need a camera in this ministry. But I don't want another Minolta. It's a good camera, but it doesn't have enough range to do what I need. What I want is a Nikon F."

This was back in the early '70s when just the body of a Nikon F was worth anywhere from $700 to $900. The two lenses I needed were worth about the same amount, so to buy the whole outfit, I might have to pay up to $1800. But I wasn't worried. I had my seed in the ground and I started getting excited. I started expecting the harvest.

## What a Deal!

Can you see what happened to me? I could have been sitting there seething over that stolen camera. I could have been sitting there getting offended, cutting myself off from the Anointing of God. But I wasn't! I had forgotten all about that thief. I was too busy being thrilled with the new camera God was giving me to worry about how the thief had done me wrong!

ONE WORD FROM GOD CAN CHANGE YOUR DESTINY

A few days later, Gloria and I were walking along the street in San Francisco when I spotted a Nikon F camera box sitting in the window of a small shop. I went in and asked the store clerk how much they wanted for it.

"We don't have a Nikon F," she answered.

"Yes, you do. It's right there in the window."

She reached over and got it, looked puzzled and carried it to a Japanese gentleman in the back of the store. "How much is this?" she asked him.

He threw up his hands and said something in Japanese that I didn't understand. So I just dug around in my pocket and found some traveler's checks. "Here," I said, "I have $250. Will you sell it to me for that?"

"OK!" said the Japanese man.

Of course I was excited about getting just the body of a Nikon F for that price. But before I had a chance to say anything about it, the store clerk dug around in a drawer, found a Nikon 50 mm lens and handed it to me along with the camera. Glory to God, my crop was coming up!

It wasn't finished yet, either. Just a few days later in another city, Gloria and I were walking along the street again and we stopped in a camera store. I looked up and noticed that way up high on the top of a display shelf there was a lens case for a Nikon 200 mm lens.

The same thing happened again. The store owner didn't know he had it, and didn't know what to charge for it. So he sold it to me for $100!

I don't mind telling you, by the time that deal was done, I was almost hoping someone would steal something from me. But then I realized, *Hey, I can give it— without someone having to steal it!* I liked that kind of harvest!

You'd like that kind of harvest too, wouldn't you?

Well, you can have it. Just start taking those opportunities for offense and planting them as seeds. Instead of crying over how badly you've been hurt, turn those hurts into harvests and start laughing at the devil. Take everything ugly he has ever thrown at you and sow it as a seed.

Begin now by praying:

"Father, in the Name of Jesus, right now I sow as seed in the kingdom of God every hurt, every bad feeling, every theft, and every evil thing any person has ever done or said to me, my family or my ministry. I release every person who has ever hurt me and I forgive them now. I lift each one of them up to You and I pray for those people. I pray, Father, that they'll come into a greater knowledge of You. I pray that their spirit be saved in the Day of the Lord.

"Now I declare before You, My God in heaven, that I expect a reward. I believe Your Word and by faith I set my sickle to my harvest. I believe I receive a hundred-fold return for every wrong deed done to me, every unkind word spoken to me and every dime stolen from me. I expect to receive a blessing of equal benefit. I claim it. It's mine and I have it now in Jesus' mighty Name!"

## Chapter 10

# Think Again! The Only Thing Powerful Enough to Keep You From Receiving Is Your Own Thinking

*Kenneth Copeland*

*"According as his divine power hath given unto us all things that pertain unto life and godliness, through the knowledge of him that hath called us to glory and virtue: Whereby are given unto us exceeding great and precious promises: that by these ye might be partakers of the divine nature...."*

— 2 Peter 1:3-4

What would you say if I asked you to tell me the biggest problem you're facing right now?

Would you say your finances? Family problems? Sickness? Job frustrations? Your weight?

If you said any of those—in fact, if you listed any circumstance at all—I have some startling news for you.

You're mistaken.

That's right, you're mistaken! I can tell you without even knowing the details of your life that, if you're a born-again believer, money is not your problem. Sickness is not your problem. Your family, weight, job, background, lack of education... none of those things is your problem.

Your problem is the way you've been thinking about those things.

"Oh now, Brother Copeland, be realistic. These are hard times. The economy is bad. The government is a mess. Everything is going downhill. Those things aren't just figments of my imagination. They're real. What difference could it possibly make how I think about them?!"

I'll show you. Look at 2 Kings 6, beginning in verse 24. There, God gives us a dramatic illustration of what a difference your thought patterns can make—even in the worst of situations. He tells us of a time when the city of Samaria was in deep trouble. An enemy king had surrounded it with fortified troops and put it under total siege. No one could go into the city and no one could go out.

"And there was a great famine in Samaria: and, behold, they besieged it, until an ass's head was sold for fourscore pieces of silver, and the fourth part of a cab of dove's dung for five pieces of silver."

(That's worse than a recession folks! It's worse than any economic depression any of us have ever seen!)

"And as the king of Israel was passing by upon the wall, there cried a woman unto him, saying, Help, my lord, O king. And he said, If the Lord do not help thee, whence shall I help thee?"

This king was saying, "Look, lady, the government is just as broke as you are. What do you expect us to do?"

"And the king said unto her, What aileth thee? And she answered, This woman said unto me, Give thy son, that we may eat him today, and we will eat my son tomorrow. So we boiled my son, and did eat him: and I said unto her on the next day, Give thy son that we may eat him: and she hath hid her *son. And it came to pass, when the king heard the words of the woman, that he rent his clothes."*

This situation had gone way beyond serious. It was pathetic, and tragically hopeless. Listen to what the king said next: *"He said, God do so and more also to me, if the head of Elisha the son of Shaphat shall stand on him this day...Behold, this evil is of the Lord; what should I wait for the Lord any longer?"*

All he knew to do was get mad at the preacher and blame the problem on God. Have you ever had thoughts like that? Well, sure you have! We all have!

But when the king sent someone to cut off Elisha's head, Elisha delivered a surprising message from the Lord. *"Then Elisha said, Hear ye the word of the Lord; Thus saith the Lord, Tomorrow about this time shall a measure of fine flour be sold for a shekel, and two measures of barley for a shekel, in the gate of Samaria"* (2 Kings 7:1).

Don't you know those words were a shock to those who heard them? Here they are in the midst of the most desperate situation they've ever seen. There's no sign of hope anywhere and the prophet of God says, "Hey, good news! This is all going to be over by tomorrow and we'll all be enjoying prosperity!"

God wasn't the one creating the disaster. He was the One with the solution to it. Yet, instead of rejoicing over this thrilling word of hope, *"...a lord on whose hand the king leaned answered the man of God, and said, Behold, if the Lord would make windows in heaven, might this thing be? And he [Elisha] said, Behold, thou shalt see it with thine eyes, but shalt not eat thereof"* (verse 2).

This man, who actually served as the "vice president" of Samaria, didn't respond to God's Word in faith. He responded to it with skepticism. He thought, *Even if God got involved, this situation is too bad to be turned around now!* His thinking was so geared toward the negative that he couldn't even imagine a positive turn of events.

As all this was going on, there were four lepers sitting outside the city's gates.

They'd been thinking negative, fear-filled thoughts just like everyone else. But then, something happened.

When Elisha spoke God's plan, the Holy Spirit moved on these men. Suddenly, their thinking changed. They didn't know it—but they began thinking the thoughts of God. *"...and they said one to another, Why sit we here until we die? If we say, We will enter into the city, then the famine is in the city, and we shall die there: and if we sit still here, we die also. Now therefore come, and let us fall unto the host of the Syrians: if they save us alive, we shall live; and if they kill us, we shall but die"* (verses 3-4).

Do you see the change in their thought pattern? Up to that time, they had been famine thinkers and leprosy thinkers. But now they were saying, "Why are we just sitting here waiting to die? Let's do something!"

When their thinking changed, their actions changed. Instead of sitting around feeling sorry for themselves, they jumped up and headed toward the Syrian camp. Do you know what they discovered when they arrived? No one was there!

The camp was abandoned. It was filled with an abundance of food and clothing and supplies—but all the soldiers were gone.

These lepers had stumbled onto a spiritual law. It's this: When hard times come, they're never as hard as they look. That's so important, I'm going to say it again. Hard times are not as hard as they look—unless you're looking in the wrong place, through the wrong eyes, thinking the wrong thoughts, and imitating the wrong people.

You may say, "But Brother Copeland, the lepers' thinking patterns didn't change that situation. God changed the situation. He made the Syrian army hear the sound of warriors coming and it scared them away!"

Exactly. But that miracle of God would never have been a blessing to those lepers—or anyone else for that matter—if they hadn't changed their thinking.

As a born-again believer, you're in much the same situation. God has already moved on your behalf. He sent Jesus to the cross to bear your sickness, weakness and pain (Isaiah 53:4-5). He healed you by His

141

stripes (1 Peter 2:24). He became poor so you could be rich (2 Corinthians 8:9). He covenanted with you to meet all your needs according to His riches in glory by Christ Jesus (Philippians 4:19).

He has given you *"all things that pertain unto life and godliness"* (2 Peter 1:3). The only thing powerful enough to keep you from receiving those things is your own thinking.

Wrong thoughts will paint the wrong pictures in your mind. They'll tell you things are worse than they are. They'll tell you that you can't do what it takes to succeed in life. But I'm here to tell you, you can succeed!

It doesn't matter how bad the economy is. People who understand money aren't afraid of hard times. In fact, it's the ungodly people who are money minded that actually wish for hard times. Such people made great fortunes back during the depression years. They bought up goods at about 10 cents on the dollar and ended up rich while others went broke.

But, of course, as believers, that's not our motive for prospering during hard times. We want to prosper in order to help others get back on top.

We want to say, "Hey friend, let me teach you how to prosper with me. Come on over here in the kingdom of God. Get over here in my house. No flood of recession or depression is going to tear it up. It's built on the Rock!" (See Matthew 7:24-26.)

If people are sick, we can say to them, "Don't let sickness and disease knock your feet out from under you, friend. Come on over here to my house. It's a healing house. By the power of God, we can show you how to be well!"

That's what the good news is really about. If we'd preach it that way instead of preaching it as some kind of religious club people need to join, they'd come running to us. If we'd preach the gospel to the poor and let them know they don't have to be poor anymore because of Jesus, they would beat down the church door just to get in there with us.

But we aren't preaching that way because we aren't thinking that way!

So, how do we change our way of thinking? God tells us in Isaiah 55:

> Seek ye the Lord while he may be found, call ye upon him while he is near: Let the wicked forsake his way, and the unrighteous man his thoughts: and let him return unto the Lord, and he will have mercy upon him; and to our God, for he will abundantly pardon. For my thoughts are not your thoughts, neither are your ways my ways, saith the Lord. For as the heavens are higher than the earth, so are my ways higher than your ways, and my thoughts than your thoughts.
>
> For as the rain cometh down, and the snow from heaven, and returneth not thither, but watereth the earth, and maketh it bring forth and bud, that it may give seed to the sower, and bread to the eater: So shall my word be that goeth forth out of my mouth: it shall not

return unto me void, but it shall
accomplish that which I please, and
it shall prosper in the thing whereto
I sent it (verses 6-11).

If we want to live the kind of life God
has in mind for us, we must trade our
thoughts for His thoughts. We must lay
down the perspectives we've gained through
past experiences and instead pick up the
wisdom of God.

Just look at what Proverbs 4 says about
the importance of that wisdom: *"Wisdom is
the principal thing; therefore get wisdom: and
with all thy getting get understanding. Exalt
her, and she shall promote thee...She shall give
to thine head an ornament of grace: a crown
of glory shall she deliver to thee"* (verses 7-9).

Acquiring the wisdom of God is the
number one top priority in our lives. Some
people think prayer is top priority. But prayer
without wisdom won't get you anywhere.

How many times have you prayed and
failed to receive your answer? It wasn't
because God missed it! The Word of God
says you ask and receive not because you

ask amiss (James 4:3). You need wisdom, you need God's thoughts about the situation before you can pray effectively.

Many times you may be crying out to God for healing when what you actually need is a miracle. You may be praying about a money shortage when what you have is a giving shortage. You may even be causing the problem yourself without knowing it.

You need God's wisdom!

How do you get it?

Jesus shows us in Luke 11:49. There, He says, *"Therefore also said the wisdom of God, I will send them prophets and apostles, and some of them they shall slay and persecute."*

Think about this for a moment. Jesus said, *"Therefore...said the wisdom of God..."* then He began to quote Scripture. He called the written Word of God the wisdom of God.

## God's Wisdom Is His Word.

Do you want to know the thoughts of God? Do you want to know the wisdom of

God? Well, go get your Bible, open it up, and read it!

If you're holding a Bible, you have God's wisdom right there in your hand.

About 20 years ago I was driving down the highway pleading with God. I had some questions I wanted to ask Him. I had some problems in my life I needed Him to address. "Oh, God," I said, "You spoke to Moses face to face. You spoke to Elijah. You spoke to Elisha. You spoke to Joshua. I want You to talk to me so badly I can hardly stand it."

Suddenly, right on the inside of me I heard His voice. *Why, Kenneth,* He said, *You have a record of everything I said to Moses. You have a record of everything I said to Joshua. You have everything I said to Elijah and Elisha. You have everything I said to Daniel and Jesus. It's lying right next to you on the seat of your car.*

I looked over and there was my Bible. I'll tell you, I shouted. "Praise God! Praise God! Praise God!"

I pulled over to the side of the road and shouted and wept with joy. I was driving an old car that had more than 98,000 miles on it (actually, it had 98,000 miles on it when I got it!) and it was leaking at every joint. At that moment, I realized that the new car I so desperately needed was laying right there on the seat by me.

The wisdom of God—all it would take for me to have that car—was right there. The wisdom of the ages was at my fingertips and I could read every word of it and stand on every word of it.

You can, too. But first, you have to be willing to forsake your old ways of thinking. *"Let the wicked forsake his way, and the unrighteous man his thoughts"* (Isaiah 55:7). Do you know what wicked means? It means twisted.

Twisted thoughts produce twisted results. Poor thinking produces poverty. Sick thinking produces sickness. You can't hold onto those kinds of thoughts and walk in the power of God.

*"For my thoughts are not your thoughts, neither are your ways my ways, saith the Lord"* (Isaiah 55:8). Let's face it. God is just plain smarter than we are. He's been around a lot longer—and what He thinks is a whole lot different than what we've been thinking.

So let the Word of God, the wisdom of God, begin to influence your thinking. Soak your mind in it. Don't just scan it lightly. Dig in it. Learn it. Take it seriously.

Then begin to pray in the spirit. Let the Spirit of God start a process of spiritual insight in your heart as you pray and worship in the spirit. After awhile, you'll begin to understand things in a new way. You'll begin to have a whole new interpretation of the problem.

You may suddenly have a realization, a deep conviction, an inner knowing. Someone may call you on the telephone and say, "I just got a word from the Lord this morning and I'm so excited about it..." And what they say is exactly what you need to hear.

However you get it, remember—wisdom is the principal thing. God's way of

149

thinking will save your life, pull you out of debt and put you on the road to prosperity. It will introduce you to possibilities you have never seen before. They're out there now...just beyond your thinking.

So quit focusing on your seemingly hopeless situation, get your Bible out, and say—just like the leper—"*Why sit we here till we die?*"!

Then get moving. There's a word full of abundance just waiting for you.

# REJOICE!

## Chapter 11

*"A merry heart doeth good like a medicine."*
— PROVERBS 17:22

*Kenneth Copeland*

With the busy schedules, high expectations and financial pressures we all face, it's easy to let joy slip through your fingers. But don't do it. Instead, get a revelation of joy that will inspire you to hang onto it all year round.

If you've recently been in many services where the Holy Spirit is moving, you've heard the laughter. You've seen, and perhaps experienced, spontaneous outbreaks of joy that range from a few quiet chuckles to uproarious laughter that literally leaves believers rolling in the aisles.

It's wonderful. There's no denying that. But what is it all about?

The answer to that question is even more thrilling than the laughter itself.

Jesus is building up His Church. He is strengthening us out of the rich treasury of His Glory. He is arming us with the spiritual might we will need to march out of every bondage and crush the devil under our feet—once and for all.

If you don't understand what all that has to do with laughter, read Nehemiah 8:10 and you'll find out. It tells us *the joy of the Lord is [our] strength.*

Many believers don't realize how literally true that verse is. So they drag around in defeat, never knowing why. "I just can't figure it out," they'll say. "I believe the Bible. I believe Jesus has set me free from this sickness...I believe He has set me free from this sin...I believe He has set me free from this lifestyle of lack. But I still can't get the victory."

The problem is, those people are too spiritually weak to receive what Jesus has given them. They need a tonic that will put some muscle back in their believing. They need something to put a sparkle in their eye, a spring in their step, and give them the spiritual might they need to knock the devil in the head and take back what belongs to them.

That's exactly what the joy of the Lord will do.

To understand why, you must realize that joy is not happiness. Happiness is a fleeting, temporal condition that depends on the comfort of your flesh. Joy, on the other hand, is a vital spiritual force. It is not based on outward circumstances, but upon the condition of your heart.

Happiness is wimpy. It disappears every time there's trouble. But joy is tough. If you'll let it, it will keep flowing in the midst of the most miserable situation. It will enable you to stand as solid as a stump until the time of trouble is over.

I realize if you're sitting there right now in the midst of trouble, you probably feel like it will never be over. But, believe me, it will!

Psalm 30:5 says, *"weeping may endure for a night, but joy cometh in the morning."* If you're a person of faith, it doesn't matter how dark conditions may seem to be right now, you can rest assured, a brighter day is on the way. That's because the devil cannot sustain an attack. He doesn't have the power. So if you'll let the force of joy keep you strong, you will outlast him and he'll eventually have to give up and admit defeat!

The Apostle Paul confirms that fact in Galatians 5:22-23. There he lists joy as a fruit of the spirit and says, *"against such there is no law."* That means there is no force in existence that can rise up and overcome the fruit of the spirit.

Here's why. The devil is not a creator. He can't come up with anything original. All he can do is take what God has made and twist it into its opposite, or reciprocal, form. Since something that's been twisted and corrupted is always weaker than it was in its original state, the devil's forces must yield when God comes on the scene. Hate must yield to love. Fear must yield to faith. Joy whips weakness and discouragement every time!

## More Than a Holy Ghost Giggle

Now let me show you how that information relates to the laughter and the outpouring of God's glory we've begun to experience.

The word *glory* as used throughout the Old Testament literally means "to be heavy laden with everything that is good," and it relates directly to the presence of God's Spirit. Some years ago, I learned from Billye Brim, who has studied Hebrew extensively, that the word *grief* is the exact opposite. It means to be heavy laden with everything that is bad.

Grief is the satanic reciprocal of glory. So, when the glory of God comes on you, grief doesn't stand a chance. It has to flee! When it does, the joy of the Lord that's in you just starts bubbling out. There's nothing to hold it back.

Of course, that's a lot of fun. We all enjoy it. But actually, the Lord is not just out to give us a good time and a Holy Ghost giggle. He has a greater purpose. He wants us to be full of joy because it's the force that will make us strong enough to carry out His plan in this final hour. It will give us the spiritual, mental and physical fortitude to rise up in the fullness of God's glory—fully healed, fully delivered, fully prosperous—so we can reap the final harvest and march out of here into the rapture.

Listen to me. The Church will not slip out of this earth in defeat and disgrace. We will not leave here like some whipped pup. No, God will take us out in glorious victory. He will do for us even more than He did for the Israelites when they left Egypt. Psalm 105 says:

> He brought them forth also with silver and gold: and there was not one feeble person among their tribes. Egypt was glad when they departed: for the fear of them fell upon them. He spread a cloud for a covering; and fire to give light in the night. The people asked, and he brought quails, and satisfied them with the bread of heaven. He opened the rock, and the waters gushed out; they ran in the dry places like a river. For he remembered his holy promise, and Abraham his servant. And he brought forth his people with joy, and his chosen with gladness (verses 37-43).

Look at that last verse again. It says God *"brought forth his people with joy."* No wonder none of them was sick or feeble! Joy made them strong from the inside out.

"Brother Copeland, are you saying joy heals?"

Yes, I am. Proverbs 17:22 plainly says, *"A merry heart doeth good like a medicine."* Even modern research has proven that joy and healing are connected. There are documented reports of people who've been healed watching old Laurel and Hardy movies. They just released a small measure of joy and their bodies responded.

## Get Another Load

The reason we haven't seen more of that kind of thing is that until recently, the Body of Christ has put very little emphasis on joy. There was even a time when we thought the more grief-stricken you were during church, the more spiritual you were.

There is nothing further from the truth. God is full of joy. Jesus is a man of joy. So if we're going to follow after Him, we'll have to be full of joy too!

Joy used to be my weakest area, spiritually. I spent so much time majoring on faith that I didn't pay much attention to it. But the Lord eventually taught me that you can't live by faith without joy.

That's because it takes strength to live by faith. We're surrounded by a world that is flowing toward death. The natural pull of it is always negative. When you leave things alone and don't work against that negative flow, they always get worse—not better. If you leave a garden unattended, it dies for lack of water or gets taken over by weeds. If you leave a house unattended, the paint peels off and the boards begin to rot.

To move toward life you must constantly swim upstream. If you ever get too weak spiritually to do that, you'll find yourself being swept back toward sickness, lack or some other form of defeat. So you can never afford to run out of strength.

No wonder the Apostle Paul wrote, *"Rejoice in the Lord always: and again I say, Rejoice"* (Philippians 4:4)! To rejoice means to re-joy, to back up your spiritual truck and get another load of it.

Paul understood the link between joy and strength. That's why he prayed for the Colossians to be *"strengthened with all might, according to [God's] glorious power, unto all patience and longsuffering with joyfulness"* (Colossians 1:11). If you were to diagram that sentence and take out the intervening phrases, you would find it actually says we are strengthened with all might with joyfulness!

Paul reaffirmed that what was true in Nehemiah's day under the Old Covenant is still true today under the New Covenant. The joy of the Lord is our strength!

## Learn to Do It Yourself

Read Colossians 1:11 again and you'll see it is that joy-inspired strength which enables us to be patient and long-suffering. (So, if you've been running short of patience lately, check your joy supply. That could be what you're lacking.)

Read Ephesians 6:10 and you'll see it takes that same strength to operate your spiritual armor. If you don't have the joy of the Lord, you'll eventually get too weak to wear it!

The fact is, joy and the strength it provides are far more vital than we ever imagined. Study Ephesians 3:16-19 and you'll see what I mean. There Paul prays:

> That [God] would grant you, according to the riches of his glory, to be strengthened with might by his Spirit in the inner man; That [the Anointed One and His Anointing] may dwell in your hearts by faith; that ye, being rooted and grounded in love, May be able to comprehend with all saints what is the breadth, and length, and depth, and height; And to know the love of [the Anointed One and His Anointing], which passeth knowledge, that ye might be filled with all the fulness of God.

According to those verses, we can't abide in the anointing without joy. We can't comprehend the love of God without joy.

We can't be filled with all the fullness of God without joy. We can't do any of those things without joy because we simply wouldn't be strong enough!

Can you see now why joy is such a major force in this end-time move of God? Even more importantly, can you see why joy must be a major force in your life if you're to be a part of that move?

"Oh yes, Brother Copeland, I do. So I'm planning to attend every Holy Ghost meeting within 100 miles of my house."

That's great. But, frankly, even if you do, it won't be enough. You see, as wonderful as it is to be in services where there is Holy Ghost laughter, you need joy all the time. And since you can't carry Kenneth E. Hagin or Rodney Howard-Browne around in your pocket, you'd better learn to release the joy of the Lord yourself!

## Start With the Word

You may not feel like you have any joy to release right now. But I can assure you,

you do. If you're a born-again child of God, you have His own joy residing in your spirit. You just need to prime the pump so it will start to flow. You need to purposely stir up the joy of the Lord.

How can you do that?

First, by meditating on the Word of God. You can understand why the Word is so important to your joy when you read some of the last things Jesus told His disciples before He went to the cross. He said:

> If ye abide in me, and my words abide in you, ye shall ask what ye will, and it shall be done unto you...If ye keep my commandments, ye shall abide in my love; even as I have kept my Father's commandments, and abide in his love. These things have I spoken unto you, that my joy might remain in you, and that your joy might be full...ask, and ye shall receive, that your joy may be full (John 15:7, 10-11, 16:24).

When you meditate on the Word of God and revelation begins to rise in your heart, joy comes! It comes because you begin to have a deeper and clearer knowledge of the Father. It comes because you realize you can go boldly before Him in prayer on the basis of the Word, and be confident your prayers will be answered.

If you've been sorrowing over a wayward child, for example, you can replace your sad thoughts with a revelation of God's promise in Isaiah 54:13, and joy will come into your heart. Suddenly, instead of crying over what the devil is doing to that child, you start shouting about what God will do. You laugh and say, "You might as well forget it, devil. Just pack it up and go home right now, because as far as I'm concerned, the victory is won. All my children shall be taught of the Lord. And great shall be the peace of my children!"

Then when the devil comes back at you and says, "Maybe so, but aren't you sorry over all the years that child has wasted?" you can shoot the Word right back at him. You can say, "No, I'm not sorry. I don't have to be sorry because Jesus bore my griefs and carried my sorrows (Isaiah 53:4). So I believe I'll just go ahead and have myself a grand time rejoicing in Him!"

Proverbs 15:23 says, *"A man hath joy by the answer of his mouth."* When you start answering the troubles and trials you're facing with the Word of God, it will release joy in you and run the devil off. He can't stand the joy of the Lord!

## Jump Into the River

Another way to stir up joy is to fellowship with the Holy Spirit. Romans 14:17 says, *"For the kingdom of God is not meat and drink; but righteousness, and peace, and joy in the Holy Ghost."*

There's joy in the Holy Ghost—so hook up with Him! Pray and sing in other tongues. Jump into the river of the Spirit with praise and thanksgiving. You may start out thinking you don't have anything to thank God for—but you'll quickly find out that you do.

You can begin by thanking Him for the blood of Jesus that has washed away your sin. You can thank Him that you're on your way to heaven. If you can't think of any other reason to praise Him, just center up on those two things. Keep shouting, "Thank God, my sins are washed away!" until joy rises up within you.

"I can't do that. I just don't feel like it."

That doesn't matter! You don't have to feel any certain way to rejoice. Joy is bigger than your emotions. In Psalm 27, King David wrote, *"And now shall mine head be lifted up above mine enemies round about me: therefore will I offer in [God's] tabernacle sacrifices of joy; I will sing, yea, I will sing praises unto the Lord (verse 6)."*

Rejoicing is an act of the will. When you don't feel like rejoicing, set your will and rejoice anyway.

If you're having financial problems, don't stay up all night worrying about how you will pay your bills. If you're going to stay up, stay up and praise God. Sing. Dance. Give thanks. Shout the Word of

God and laugh at the devil until joy comes. Then keep on rejoicing until you're so filled with the strength and might of God that nothing can stop you.

Keep on rejoicing until your body is well. Keep on rejoicing until every chain the devil has used to keep you in bondage snaps like a thread. Keep on rejoicing until people start coming to you—and they will!— saying, "Hey, I want some of that joy! Can you tell me how to get it?"

Think about it. Wouldn't it be wonderful if we started rejoicing and just kept on rejoicing every day from now on until this whole earth was filled with the Glory of God? I believe with all my heart that's what God is calling us to do.

Let's get on with it so we can rejoice our way right into the rapture.

Let's rejoice in the Lord, always. And again I say, rejoice!

## Prayer for Salvation and Baptism in the Holy Spirit

Heavenly Father, I come to You in the Name of Jesus. Your Word says, *"Whosoever shall call on the name of the Lord shall be saved"* (Acts 2:21). I am calling on You. I pray and ask Jesus to come into my heart and be Lord over my life according to Romans 10:9. *"...if thou shalt confess with thy mouth the Lord Jesus, and shalt believe in thine heart that God hath raised him from the dead, thou shalt be saved."* I do that now. I confess that Jesus is Lord, and I believe in my heart that God raised Him from the dead.

I am now reborn! I am a Christian—a child of Almighty God! I am saved! You also said in Your Word, *"If ye then, being evil, know how to give good gifts unto your children: HOW MUCH MORE shall your heavenly Father give the Holy Spirit to them that ask him?"* (Luke 11:13). I'm also asking You to fill me with the Holy Spirit. Holy Spirit, rise up within me as I praise God. I fully expect to speak with other tongues as You give me the utterance (Acts 2:4).

Begin to praise God for filling you with the Holy Spirit. Speak those words and syllables you receive—not in your own language, but the language given to you by the Holy Spirit. You have to use your own voice. God will not force you to speak. Worship and praise Him in your heavenly language—in other tongues.

Continue with the blessing God has given you and pray in tongues each day.

You are a born-again, Spirit-filled believer. You'll never be the same!

Find a good Word of God preaching church, and become a part of a church family who will love and care for you as you love and care for them.

We need to be hooked up to each other. It increases our strength in God. It's God's plan for us.

# Books Available From Kenneth Copeland Publications

**by Kenneth Copeland**
* A Ceremony of Marriage
  A Matter of Choice
  Covenant of Blood
  Faith and Patience—The Power Twins
* Freedom From Fear
  Giving and Receiving
  Honor—Walking in Honesty, Truth and Integrity
  How to Conquer Strife
  How to Discipline Your Flesh
  How to Receive Communion
  Living at the End of Time—A Time of Supernatural
     Increase
  Love Never Fails
  Managing God's Mutual Funds
* Now Are We in Christ Jesus
* Our Covenant With God
* Prayer—Your Foundation for Success
  Prosperity: The Choice Is Yours
  Rumors of War
* Sensitivity of Heart
  Six Steps to Excellence in Ministry
  Sorrow Not! Winning Over Grief and Sorrow
* The Decision Is Yours
* The Force of Faith
* The Force of Righteousness
  The Image of God in You
  The Laws of Prosperity
* The Mercy of God
  The Miraculous Realm of God's Love
  The Outpouring of the Spirit—The Result of Prayer
* The Power of the Tongue
  The Power to Be Forever Free

The Troublemaker
* The Winning Attitude
Turn Your Hurts Into Harvests
* Welcome to the Family
* You Are Healed!
Your Right-Standing With God

**by Gloria Copeland**
* And Jesus Healed Them All
Are You Ready?
Build Your Financial Foundation
Build Yourself an Ark
Fight On!
God's Prescription for Divine Health
God's Success Formula
God's Will for You
God's Will for Your Healing
God's Will Is Prosperity
* God's Will Is the Holy Spirit
* Harvest of Health
Hidden Treasures
Living Contact
* Love—The Secret to Your Success
No Deposit—No Return
Pleasing the Father
Pressing In—It's Worth It All
The Power to Live a New Life
The Unbeatable Spirit of Faith
* Walk in the Spirit
Walk With God
Well Worth the Wait

**Books Co-Authored by Kenneth and Gloria Copeland**
Family Promises
Healing Promises
Prosperity Promises

From Faith to Faith—A Daily Guide to Victory
Over the Edge—Youth Devotional
Pursuit of His Presence—Daily Devotional

## Other Books Published by KCP

The First 30 Years—A Journey of Faith
The story of the lives of Kenneth and
Gloria Copeland.
Real People. Real Needs. Real Victories.
A book of testimonies to encourage your faith.

John G. Lake—His Life, His Sermons, His Boldness
of Faith
The Holiest of All by Andrew Murray
The New Testament in Modern Speech by
Richard Francis Weymouth

## Products Designed by KCP and Heirborne™ for Today's Children and Youth

Baby Praise Board Book
Noah's Ark Coloring Book
The *Shout!* Super-Activity Book
The SWORD Adventure Book

* Available in Spanish

# World Offices of
# Kenneth Copeland Ministries

For more information about KCM and a free
catalog, please write the office nearest you:

Kenneth Copeland Ministries
Fort Worth, Texas  76192-0001

Kenneth Copeland Ministries
Locked Bag 2600
Mansfield Delivery Centre
QUEENSLAND 4122
AUSTRALIA

Kenneth Copeland Ministries
Post Office Box 15
BATH
BA1  1GD
ENGLAND

Kenneth Copeland Ministries
Private Bag X 909
FONTAINEBLEAU
2032
REPUBLIC OF
   SOUTH AFRICA

Kenneth Copeland Ministries
Post Office Box 378
Surrey
BRITISH COLUMBIA
V3T  5B6
CANADA

UKRAINE
L'VIV  290000
Post Office Box 84
Kenneth Copeland Ministries
L'VIV  290000
UKRAINE

# We're Here for You!

Join Kenneth and Gloria Copeland, and the *Believer's Voice of Victory* broadcast, Monday through Friday and on Sunday each week, and learn how faith in God's Word can take your life from ordinary to extraordinary.

It's some of the most in-depth teaching you'll ever hear on subjects like faith and healing, deliverance and prosperity, protection and hope. And it's all designed to get you where you want to be—*on top!* The teachings are by some of today's best-known ministers, including Kenneth and Gloria Copeland, Jerry Savelle, Charles Capps, Creflo A. Dollar Jr., Kellie Copeland and Edwin Louis Cole.

So, whether it's before breakfast, during lunch or after a long day at the office, plan to make *Believer's Voice of Victory* a daily part of your life. And see for yourself how *One Word From God* can change your life forever.

You can catch the *Believer's Voice of Victory* broadcast on the following cable and satellite channels:

| | |
|---|---|
| Sunday<br>9-9:30 p.m. ET<br>Cable*/G5,<br>Channel 3—TBN | Monday through Friday<br>7-7:30 p.m. ET<br>Cable*/G1,<br>Channel 17—INSP |
| Monday through Friday<br>6-6:30 a.m. ET<br>Cable*/G5,<br>Channel 7—WGN | Monday through Friday<br>11-11:30 a.m. ET<br>Cable*/G5,<br>Channel 3—TBN |
| Monday through Friday<br>6:30-7 a.m. ET<br>Cable*/G5,<br>Channel 20—BET | Monday through Friday<br>6:30-7 a.m. ET<br>Cable*/W1,<br>Channel 7—Cornerstone TV |

*Check your local listing for more times and stations in your area.

## Believer's Voice of Victory

Nowhere else will you get a monthly dose of the inspired teaching and encouragement of Kenneth and Gloria Copeland than in the issues of the *Believer's Voice of Victory* magazine. Also included are real-life testimonies of God's miraculous power and divine intervention into the lives of people just like you! Featured guest ministers offer their latest revelation and godly instruction to encourage your faith.

If you would like to receive a FREE subscription to *Believer's Voice of Victory,* just send your name and address to:

Kenneth Copeland Ministries
Fort Worth, Texas  76192-0001
**It's more than just a magazine—it's a ministry.**

## *Shout!*

## ...The faith-filled magazine just for kids!

*Shout! The Voice of Victory for Kids* is a Word-charged, action-packed, bimonthly magazine that's available FREE to kids everywhere!

Featuring *Wichita Slim* and *Commander Kellie and the Superkids*sm, *Shout!* is filled with colorful adventure comics, challenging games and puzzles, exciting short stories, solve-it-yourself mysteries and much more!!

So if you or some of your friends would like to receive a FREE subscription to *Shout!,* just send each kid's name, date of birth and complete address to:

Kenneth Copeland Ministries
Fort Worth, Texas  76192-0001

Or call:

1-800-359-0075
(9 a.m.-5 p.m. CT)

**Stand up, sign up and get ready to *Shout!***

## The Harrison House Vision

Proclaiming the truth and the power
Of the Gospel of Jesus Christ
With excellence;
Challenging Christians to
Live victoriously,
Grow spiritually,
Know God intimately.